The
Glorious Fourth

THE GLORIOUS FOURTH
An American Holiday, An American History

Diana Karter Appelbaum

Facts On File
New York • Oxford

NI

The Glorious Fourth: An American Holiday, An American History

Facts On File, Inc.
460 Park Avenue South
New York, New York 10016
USA

Library of Congress Cataloging-in-Publication Data

Appelbaum, Diana Karter
  The glorious fourth.

  Includes index.
  1. Fourth of July celebrations.   I. Title.
E286.A125   1989   394.2'684   88-30881
ISBN 0-8160-1767-0

British CIP data available on request
Facts On File books are available at special discounts when purchased in bulk quantities for businesses, associations, institutions, or sales promotion. Please contact the Special Sales Department of our New York office at 212/683-2244 (dial 800/322-8755 except in NY, AK or HI).

Text Design by Ron Monteleone

Jacket Design by Catherine Hyman

Composition by Facts On File, Inc.

Printed in the United States of America

10 9 8 7 6 5 4 3 2 1

Contents

*To my parents
Elizabeth and Peter Karter*

Introduction

When I was a small girl in Norwalk, Connecticut, our family went every year to see the Fourth of July fireworks at Calf Pasture, the town beach. On summer afternoons, the beach was a familiar place of hot sand, seashells and gentle waves. We never went to the beach at night except on the Fourth of July, and it was very different then. The sand was damp and cold. You couldn't see the waves at night; you could only hear them. We sat on my father's old army blanket, but the damp chill crept right through the closely woven olive-drab wool, and my sisters and I had to be bundled in sweaters to keep warm. Some years I fell asleep on the blanket before the fireworks were over. I was certainly always asleep in the back of the station wagon before we got home—but no one ever suggested that we not go.

I take my children every year to see the fireworks at our town beach at Lake Massapoag in Sharon, Massachusetts. We walk to the lake along a wooded road illuminated at intervals by dazzling bursts of light from Roman candles. Every year the fireworks display is better than the year before, better than any previous year, ever—and we wouldn't miss it for the world.

It is part of the essence of holidays to do on them things that we recall doing when we were children, and to know that our grandchildren will celebrate the holiday in some of the same ways. Continuity, the certainty that key elements remain unchanged from year to year, makes these days valuable loadstones in a changing world.

Yet the truth about our holidays is that they change more than they remain the same. A few practices, transmitted from one generation to the next, remind us of the continuity of our cultural traditions. Others, newly introduced, reflect the preoccupations of contemporary society. Thanksgiving Day, the American holiday that seems unchanged from time out of memory, began as a day of worship in a Puritan colony and was transformed into a harvest festival, homecoming and feast day by the Puritan's prosperous rural descendants. Today it is a feast day, homecoming and ritual celebration of the game of football. Every generation celebrates holidays in a manner consistent with its desires.

The Fourth of July has changed to reflect the changing nature of American society. It has been imperialist and nostalgic, frivolous and political, drunken and teetotal, but always, it has been an accurate mirror of the mood of the American people. This book is an exploration of the changing ways in which Americans have celebrated the glorious Fourth, a chronicle of this triumphant national holiday.

1776   1

On July 2, 1776, in the dark hours before dawn, Caesar Rodney rode through rain and thunder toward Philadelphia. He arrived mud-spattered and weary, but in time to cast the deciding vote for independence. Rodney's arrival brought the tally to 12 colonies in favor of independence, one colony abstaining, none opposed. On that July day a nation was born.

The Seeds of Independence

The United States of America had been in gestation for a long time. Arguably, the process of forming a nation began with the intercolonial congress held to protest the Stamp Act in 1765, but the movement toward independence was pushed forward most rapidly by the Boston Port Bill and the other "Intolerable Acts" voted by the British Parliament in 1774. Then, on the nineteenth of April in 1775, regular British troops fired on colonial militia at Lexington and Concord in Massachusetts. War had begun, but a question remained: was this war the rebellion of a people pressing their legitimate sovereign for a redress of grievances? Or was it a "War of Independence"?

Most Americans in the spring of 1775 thought of George III as their rightful king. The British Parliament, it was increasingly agreed, lacked the right to legislate for colonists, who were as entitled as other British subjects to vote for their own legislators. Many colonists who would later favor independence continued, even after the fighting had begun, to hope that the British government would recognize the legitimacy of the colonies' claim to be self-governing commonwealths under the Crown—but not under Parliament.

The Second Continental Congress convened in Philadelphia on May 10, 1775. The date was set when Congress adjourned the previous year, but the fighting at Lexington and Concord changed everything. The First Continental Congress had petitioned the British government with documents advocating the rights of Americans and had instituted an embargo on trade with England in an effort to use economic pressure to win political liberties. The Second Congress was a de facto government fighting a war against England.[1] On May 17, while still trying to formulate a response to the events at Lexington and Concord, Congress received news that Ethan Allen and 83 Green Mountain Boys had captured Fort Ticonderoga on Lake Champlain from the British garrison. Here, Americans had taken the offensive. Less than a month after the fighting began, American colonists were behaving like citizens of an independent nation at war with a foreign power. For the next year, Congress would act like the government of a sovereign nation while refusing to admit, even to itself, that it was doing so.

Encamped around Boston was an army of colonial militia, gathered in response to the British march on Concord. On June 14, Congress created the Continental Army and the next day named George Washington of Virginia commanding general. In the months after creating the army, Congress began to issue currency, took steps to arrange for the importation of munitions, sent commissioners to negotiate treaties with Indian tribes, established a postal service, granted letters of marque authorizing American privateers to attack British shipping, ordered the creation of a navy and made diplomatic contact with France—all actions of a sovereign nation, not a colony.

Most Americans who supported the Congress in the winter of 1775–76 thought of themselves as being in active and well-justified rebellion against their rightful king. They hoped that the king would install a new government and institute new policies, but still remain their sovereign—for government without the king, the English king, was unthinkable. Three-quarters of the colonists were descended from English families. Their Bible, their prayer books and their schoolbooks were written in English. The history they learned and the heroes, saints and martyrs they revered were English. The very rights the colonists were fighting for were the rights of Englishmen and, long after the point when it seems apparent to a modern observer that the tie had been irrevocably broken, they continued to think of themselves as Englishmen.

Liberty or Loyalty?

Thomas Paine arrived in America only two years before he published *Common Sense* in January 1776. The pamphlet, published anonymously, was a powerful argument for independence. Paine did what almost no American had previously been willing to do: he attacked "not only the tyranny, but the tyrant, . . ." calling on Americans to reject King George as they had rejected Parliament and asserting that only independence could secure and guarantee American liberty.

Paine argued that the kings of England did not rule by divine right and wrote persuasively of the prospects for forming an independent government without any king at all. Americans, many of whom had hesitated to think such thoughts even as they had gone about the business of setting up independent governments, found in *Common Sense* an ideological justification for their actions. The pamphlet was read in every city and hamlet in the colonies. It was read in taverns and at hearthside, denounced by furious loyalists and praised by friends of liberty, among whom it set in motion a groundswell of support for independence. On April 12, 1776, the Provincial Congress of North Carolina authorized its delegates at Philadelphia to vote for independence. North Carolina was the first colony to vote such an authorization, but the news would not reach Philadelphia for several weeks.

John Adams, who was justly called "the Atlas on whose shoulders independence rested" by his fellow delegate Richard Stockton of New Jersey, had long been prepared to make the final break with England. On May 10 Congress authorized Adams to write the preamble to a congressional resolution calling on the people of those individual colonies that had not yet established new governments to do so. Adams took the opportunity to write a paragraph repudiating allegiance to the Crown, which met with heated opposition, but passed by a narrow margin.

In every colony, even in Massachusetts and Virginia where revolutionary ardor was most fervent, there were many individuals loyal to England, and still more who urged moderation. In the middle colonies, the moderates and loyalists may have been a majority and many prominent citizens could be counted among their ranks. Massachusetts and Virginia were ripe for independence in the spring of 1776, but New York, Pennsylvania, New Jersey, Maryland, Delaware and South Carolina were not. If one vote would have been allowed to every freeman in the colonies, independence would probably have lost. But the Continental Congress did not represent all opinions equally. Each year since 1774, the Congress had increasingly taken on the complexion of a rebel assembly, and the governments newly formed in each colony were, likewise, governments of rebellion. The question was whether those Americans in active rebellion against English rule were prepared to declare themselves independent.

Some observers then and since have pointed out that declaring independence at this point, when America was already at war with England, was like the action of a man who quits his job after he has been fired. But to the Americans of 1776 the act of declaring independence from Britain was a grave step. Colonists who had always known themselves to be Englishmen would now have to think of themselves as something else. And any lingering hope of negotiating with the Crown for a satisfactory redress of grievances would have to be abandoned. Once independence was declared, the war would have to be fought to the point of victory or, what seemed more likely to many, defeat.

The Moment of Truth Arrives

Despite these reasons for postponing indefinitely a decision on independence, a formal declaration was becoming a pressing necessity. America needed foreign aid to win the war, and no foreign power was likely to aid a rebellion that aimed at mere reconciliation with the mother country on improved terms. A revolution that severed America from England, permanently lessening British power, was, on the other hand, a goal that rival European states might find worth supporting.

In order to be credible and useful in obtaining foreign aid, independence had to be the unanimous will of delegations from all 13 colonies and, even then, success would require sufficient popular support to back up the brave words of a Congressional declaration. So Congress waited anxiously in the spring of 1776 for signs that the people wanted independence.

On May 15, the Virginia Convention meeting in Williamsburg declared itself independent of Great Britain and instructed the Virginia delegates in Congress to propose a resolution declaring the "United colonies free and independent States." On May 27 the Virginia resolution was laid before Congress alongside North Carolina's instructions to its delegates to vote for independence, and there it lay for several days while Congress worked on the details of a plan of defense that General Washington had helped to design and would soon implement. Finally, on June 7, Richard Henry Lee of Virginia offered a three-part resolution:

That these United Colonies are, and of a right ought to be, free and independent States, that they are absolved from all allegiance to the British Crown, and that all political connection between them and the state of Great Britain is, and ought to be, totally dissolved.

That it is expedient forthwith to take the most effectual measures for forming foreign Alliances.

That a plan of confederation be prepared and transmitted to the respective Colonies for their consideration and approbation.

The moment of truth had arrived, but the delegates could not make up their minds. For three days Congress dithered—before finally reaching a decision on June 10 to postpone consideration of the matter until July 1. Three weeks, it was hoped, would allow those provincial assemblies still debating independence to give their delegations clear instructions on the question.

The faction favoring independence did manage to obtain the appointment of a committee to draft a declaration of independence in order "that no time be lost, in case the Congress agree thereto." The members of this committee were John Adams, Benjamin Franklin, Roger Sherman, Robert R. Livingston and Thomas Jefferson.

Delegates from New Hampshire, New York and Maryland sent messages to their home colonies requesting that a decision be reached on independence and that appropriate instructions be sent. On June 14, the Pennsylvania Assembly framed new instructions to its delegation, authorizing the members to follow their own judgment in voting on measures necessary to promote the liberty, safety and interests of America. Not satisfied with this, the radical element set up a new provincial conference, which instructed the Pennsylvania delegation to concur in a congressional vote for independence. Pennsylvania delegates now had to decide not only how to vote, but whether the old assembly or the new conference was the legitimate government of Pennsylvania.

On June 14, the Delaware House of Assembly, like the Pennsylvania Assembly, instructed its delegates to do what they thought best when the issue came to a vote. On June 15 the Provincial Congress of New Jersey ousted the governor, Benjamin Franklin's loyalist son, William, and sent new delegates to Philadelphia with instructions to vote for independence, if they deemed it to be necessary or expedient. Connecticut, already presumed to be in the independence camp, formally instructed its delegation to vote for independence on June 14 and New Hampshire followed suit on June 15.

Maryland and New York still hesitated. When the Maryland Convention assembled on June 21, it sent a message to Congress requesting that the vote be put off beyond July to allow more time for debate; Congress responded that the date was set. Maryland proceeded to depose its last royal governor and, on Friday, June 29, voted yes on the great question. On Monday, July 1, 1776, the resolution of the Maryland Convention in hand, Congress resolved itself into a committee of the whole to consider voting for independence.

Eager expectation changed to consternation when several delegations failed to vote as expected. Each delegation had a single vote. Pennsylvania and South Carolina voted no. There were two delegates from Delaware—one voted yes and one voted no. New York, still awaiting instructions from home, abstained. So, in place of the anticipated unanimity for independence, there was a 9-3-1 split.

At this point, Edward Rutledge of South Carolina rose to speak. Although he personally believed that a vote for independence was premature and had led the South Carolina delegation in voting no, Rutledge offered to change his vote on the following day for the sake of unanimity. Congress agreed to take the issue up again on the morning of July 2.

The New York abstention could be construed as not contravening unanimity, on the assumption that the New York Assembly would eventually decide for independence, but the votes of Pennsylvania and Delaware were essential. There were seven delegates from Pennsylvania, three favoring independence, four opposing, all authorized to vote their consciences. John Dickinson and Robert Morris, unwilling to vote for independence, agreed to absent themselves when the vote was taken on July 2nd, changing the Pennsylvania vote to "aye."

George Read and Thomas McKean of Delaware were deadlocked. Read, a patriot who later signed the Declaration, thought that passage on July 2 was premature. Caesar Rodney, a brigadier general in the militia and the third member of the delegation, was in Delaware looking into a threatened loyalist uprising in Sussex County when the vote took place. When an urgent message from Thomas McKean reached Rodney at his home in Dover, he mounted his horse and began his celebrated 80-mile ride to Philadelphia, arriving in time to cast the decisive vote for independence. The resolution passed late in the afternoon of July 2, 1776; the vote was 12 colonies to none, with New York not voting.

John Adams was elated. "Yesterday," he wrote to his wife, Abigail, on July 3, "the greatest question was decided, which ever was debated in America, and a greater, perhaps, never was nor will be decided among men." Later on the same day, he wrote a second letter to his beloved Abigail:

> The second day of July, 1776, will be the most memorable epocha in the history of America. I am apt to believe that it will be celebrated by succeeding generations as the great anniversary Festival. It ought to be commemorated, as the day of deliverance, by solemn acts of devotion to God Almighty. It ought to be solemnized with pomp and parade, with shows, games, sports, guns, bells, bonfires, and illuminations, from one end of this continent to the other, from this time forward, forevermore.[2]

Artist John Trumbull drew each of the signers from life for his famous picture of the United States declaring independence. (The Declaration on Independence, John Trumbull, courtesy of Yale University Art Gallery)

John Adams was correct, albeit somewhat ahead of events. Adams, who had been waiting impatiently for Congress to declare independence for over a year, had to wait another two days while the delegates debated the wording of the declaration and formalized the resolution that they had passed. The Great Anniversary Festival would be celebrated forevermore not on the day when Congress voted for independence, but on the day when Congress concluded a careful review of the wording and formally issued its declaration

A Declaration

Five men had been appointed to write a Declaration of Independence. In the end, it was written by the pen of a single man. How Thomas Jefferson came to write the Declaration will never be entirely clear, since the Continental Congress recorded only its resolutions; no one kept notes of congressional debates, much less the discussions of congressional committees. In 1822 Adams wrote down his recollections of how Jefferson was chosen:

Jefferson proposed to me to make the draught.
I said, "I will not."
"You should do it!"
"Oh! no."
"Why will you not? You ought to do it."
"I will not."
"Why?"
"Reasons enough."
"What can be your reasons?"
"Reason first—You are a Virginian, and a Virginian ought to appear at the head of this business. Reason second—I am obnoxious, suspected, and unpopular. You are very much otherwise. Reason third—You can write ten times better than I can."

When Adams recorded this conversation, he was an old man recalling events nearly 50 years in the past, yet, whether or not the conversation took place precisely as he recalled it, the arguments advanced are all true. In July 1776, John Adams was one of the most prominent leaders of the Revolution and the leading exponent of independence; it was indeed logical, as Jefferson maintained, that he ought to have written the declaration. Yet he was and would always be unpopular, and he was from Massachusetts. Since Massachusetts had suffered the most from British occupation and attacks, its citizens had been goaded into a greater eagerness for independence than those of any other colony; it was better politics to let the declaration be written by someone from another

A contemporary English engraving of the Declaration of Independence being read in an American city. (Barnard's New Complete History of England)

FIRST READING OF THE DECLARATION OF INDEPENDENCE IN NEW YORK. —[Drawn by A. R. Waud.]

An artist's conception of the first reading of the Declaration of Independence at New York.
(Harper's Weekly, *July 9, 1870, p. 433.*)

state. Virginia was the obvious choice, both because it was one of the largest colonies and because it was Virginia that had proposed the resolution.

Jefferson was a brilliant writer. It has been said that had the irrepressible Franklin written the Declaration, he would have peppered it with jokes. A declaration from the pen of Adams would have been erudite, contentious and turgid. The Declaration prepared by Jefferson was noble in sentiment, brilliant in word.

Following the July 2 vote for independence, Congress took two days to consider carefully the wording of Mr. Jefferson's draft for a declaration. This was the document that would present America's case to the world, most particularly, it was intended to persuade France to enter the war as an ally. The arguments and the wording of the document were therefore crucial to the American cause. Fortunately, the delegates did not tamper excessively with Jefferson's language. Most of the emendations improved the text in minor ways, but there were two major alterations: a passage criticizing the people of England was struck by delegates who hoped to retain the goodwill of some of the British public, even while they fought the government, and Jefferson's attack on the slave trade was deleted when it became clear that some Southern delegates would not vote for a declaration that criticized slavery.

The First Days of Independence

Debate of Jefferson's declaration was closed on the evening of July 4, 1776, and America officially became an independent nation. In years to come, the Fourth of July would be celebrated as the American Independence Day, but in 1776 the immediate task was to notify the people of the colonies and the world that Congress had declared independence from Great Britain. To that end, John Dunlap, a Philadelphia printer, was requested to produce a number of copies of the Declaration for dispatch to the colonial assemblies, conventions and committees of safety and to the Continental Army. These were sent out beginning on July 5. Since the abstention of New York stopped the Declaration from being unanimous, it was first printed under the heading "A Declaration by the Representatives of the United States in General Congress Assembled," and went out over the signatures of John Hancock, President, and Charles Thomson, Secretary of the Congress. Only several months after the Declaration was voted upon and issued would delegates be asked to affix their signatures to an official copy.[3]

Philadelphia, which naturally learned the news first, arranged a celebration for Monday, July 8.[4] This was also the date of Independence celebrations in Easton, Pennsylvania and Trenton, New Jersey. John Nixon, a member of the

A pro-Independence mob tears the statue of King George from its pedestal on the Battery in New York. (From an old print in the collection of the New-York Historical Society)

Black and white Americans raise a liberty pole as a well-dressed Tory turns away. In the background, men enlist in the Continental Army and a crowd rips the image of George III from a tavern sign as the militia drills and prepares to fire cannon salutes. (Raising the Liberty Pole, engraving by John C. McRae, 1875, after a painting by F.A. Chapman. Library of Congress)

Committee of Safety, read the Declaration to a crowd gathered in the yard of the Pennsylvania State House, a building known to posterity as Independence Hall. Bells rang all day long; the militia paraded on the Common and fired salutes, despite the shortage of powder. Crowds in the streets celebrated the final separation from British authority and they did so graphically—by burning the king's heraldic arms. The painted wooden carving of the king's arms was taken down from the State House and carried to the Common, where empty casks had been stacked up to burn it in a glorious, patriotic bonfire.

The copy of the Declaration sent to General Washington on July 6, reached him in camp at New York on July 9. At six o'clock, each brigade was drawn up on its parade ground to hear the Declaration read and respond with three huzzahs. The people of New York responded more volubly.

In 1770, the New York legislature, celebrating the repeal of the Stamp Act, had erected a handsome, life-size, equestrian statue of George III, the first equestrian statue in the colonies. It was placed near the fort on the Battery, on a small elliptical lawn surrounded by an iron rail. The statue itself was made of gilded lead and stood on a handsome marble pedestal, a tribute to New York's mercantile prosperity and the magnificence of the British monarchy. When news of the Declaration reached New York on July 9, King George was pulled from his pedestal, roughly dismembered and sent off to Litchfield, Connecticut to be melted down and turned into some 42,000 lead bullets, later fired at His Majesty's troops.

Patriots in other towns who had no statues to topple did the best they could with materials on hand. Towns large enough to have a courthouse tore the king's coat of arms off the courthouse wall and burned it on a bonfire. In New York City and Dover, Delaware, portraits of the king were burned. Other towns, lacking actual portraits, burned King George in effigy, and in more than one town signboards from taverns called "The King's Arms" were thrown onto the fires. Everywhere, the Declaration was read by a leading local patriot to resounding cheers, while in some towns disaffected Tories stood quietly at the edges of the crowd. Bells rang through the day when the Declaration was read; guards of honor fired volleys and the militia paraded. The Declaration was received with enthusiasm and relief, for it eliminated the stress inherent in fighting a "loyal" rebellion. As one New Jersey patriot put it in a letter to his cousin: "I could hardly own the King and fight against him at the same time; but now these matters are cleared up. Heart and hand shall move together." [5]

Notes

1. For the Actions of the Continental Congress in the debate on independence, I have relied on Edmund Cody Burnett, *The Continental Congress*, The Macmillan Company, New York, 1941.

2. John Adams's famous letters on independence can be found in *The Adams Family Correspondence*, Volume 2, L. H. Butterfield, editor, the Belknap Press of Harvard University Press, Cambridge, Massachusetts, 1963, pp. 27–33.

3. Burnett; also, Dumas Malone, *The Story of the Declaration of Independence*, Oxford University Press, New York, 1954.

4. *Extracts from the Diary of Christopher Marshall, Kept in Philadelphia and Lancaster During the American Revolution, 1774–1781*, edited by William Duane, Joel Munsell, Albany, 1877; *Adams Family Correspondence*, edited by L.H. Butterfield, Volume 2, The Belknap Press of Harvard University Press, Cambridge, 1963; *The New York Gazette and Weekly Mercury*, July 15, 1776 and July 22, 1776; *The Virginia Gazette* (Williamsburg), July 29, 1776; Charles D. Deshler, "How the Declaration was Received in the Old Thirteen," *Harper's New Monthly Magazine, July 1892; The Writings of George Washington from the Original Manuscript Sources, 1745–1799*, edited by John C. Fitzpatrick, U.S. Government Printing Office, Washington, 1931–1944, Volume 5, pp. 244-125; and *Celebration by the Inhabitants of Worcester, Massachusetts, of the Centennial Anniversary of the Declaration of Independence, July 4, 1876, To which are added Historical and Chronological Notes*, Printed by order of the City Council, Worcester, 1876.

5. Letter from Joseph Barton, Sussex County, New Jersey, July 9, 1776, quoted in "How the Declaration was Received in the Old Thirteen," Charles D. Deshler, *Harper's New Monthly Magazine*, July 1892, page 169.

Revolutionary
Celebrations   2

It was a fine, brave thing to declare independence, but quite another to prove the bold words by actually defeating His Majesty's forces in war. Seven weeks after independence was proclaimed and celebrated, New York fell to the British and Washington was forced to retreat, with a much reduced army, into New Jersey. Washington's stunning Christmas victory over the Hessians at Trenton lifted American spirits, but with thousands of British troops on American soil, the rebellious colonies were still a long way from real independence. Most Americans appear to have viewed July 4, 1777 as one more day in a long and difficult war. It required vision and dedication to see the day as the first anniversary of what would someday become a great and independent nation— but a handful of patriots did see it that way.

The First Anniversary

Congress agreed to adjourn on the anniversary of Independence and hold a dinner. On the morning of the fourth, all ships of the little United States Navy that were then in Philadelphia lined up in the river. Sailors climbed into the rigging, standing in neat rows on the yards and making a fine appearance that impressed John Adams, ever an admirer of military spit and polish. President Hancock and several members of Congress were saluted with 13 guns as they went aboard the warship *Delaware*. At the dinner, Congress was entertained by a Hessian army band captured at Trenton and patriotic toasts were punctuated with volleys fired by the troops. Newly raised troops from Maryland and North Carolina, who happened to be passing through Philadelphia on their way to join the Army, paraded in the afternoon. Bells rang through the day, bonfires blazed in the streets at night, and a display of fireworks concluded with 13 rockets. Toward evening there was a spontaneous illumination, as the citizens of Philadelphia lit candles in their windows, except for a very few surly Tories whose windows remained dark.[1]

In ardently revolutionary and ever-devout Boston, the Reverend William Gordon of Roxbury was invited to preach a Fourth of July sermon to the members of the General Court.[2] There was a militia parade and salutes were fired by ships in Boston Harbor.[3]

At Portsmouth, New Hampshire, the anniversary of American Independence was celebrated at the initiative of Captain Thompson, commander of a Continental frigate in the harbor. He invited "all true friends to American Independency" to lunch aboard ship, where they toasted "Prosperity, Freedom and Independency" and heard a 13-gun salute. Answering salutes were fired by a French ship and a Portsmouth privateer. The people of Portsmouth, who had planned no celebration, stood on the wharves to watch the salutes being fired.[4]

Providence, Rhode Island celebrated by firing cannon,[5] while in Charleston, South Carolina, the day was celebrated in style. At sunrise, the American flag was displayed from all of the forts, batteries and vessels of Charleston Harbor, as every bell in the city rang in the day. The Charles-Town regiment of militia and the Charles-Town Artillery Company assembled on the parade grounds, where they were reviewed by the president of South Carolina and members of the Privy Council. At one o'clock, the harbor forts, beginning with Fort Moultrie on Sullivan's Island, discharged 76 pieces of cannon, after which the militia fired three rounds.

The president, members of the legislature, public officials, clergymen, military officers and other gentlemen of note then attended a dinner in the Council Chamber, which concluded with 13 toasts. The first toast was to "the Free, Independent and Sovereign States of America." The next was to General

Washington, then to the Fourth of July 1776 and on down the patriotic list, with each of the 13 toasts followed by a 13-gun artillery salute. Toasts of this sort were a convention of the formal dinners of the era. The wording and order of the toasts were arranged in advance, and often printed on the program. The privilege of delivering each toast was an honor. Only after all of these "set" toasts had been offered and drunk would individuals rise to offer spontaneous toasts. The Charleston celebration concluded with an evening candlelight illumination of the town.[6]

In most towns and villages and in the camps of the Continental Army the day passed unmarked, it apparently having occurred to very few people that the anniversary ought to be celebrated until they read in the papers of celebrations in Portsmouth, Philadelphia, Boston and Charleston. Other dates, however, were commemorated by some Revolutionary era patriots. Citizens of Boston held an annual commemoration of the Boston Massacre. The initial commemoration was held on the first anniversary of the massacre, March 5, 1771, and a ceremony with an appropriate oration was held every year until 1783. During the British occupation of Boston, the commemoration was held by exiled patriots at Watertown. In 1783, the Boston town meeting voted to discontinue the Boston Massacre commemoration and substitute the official celebration of July Fourth.[7]

Establishing the Date

Later chroniclers have asked: Why the fourth of July? Why not celebrate American Independence on April nineteenth, when fighting began at Lexington? Or on July second, when the vote for independence was taken? John Adams, in his prescient letter predicting that the event would be celebrated "from this time forward, forevermore," had expected celebrations to be held on the second of July. It might have been even more appropriate to wait until independence was won and celebrate the anniversary of the victory. But to wait until victory was won would not have assisted in the winning of that victory.

The American Revolution was a long, discouraging war. It was a war of retreats and of skirmishes, of long periods of retrenchment between major battles, and of flagging enthusiasm for a cause that depended upon the voluntary support of the citizenry to succeed. Public celebrations of American independence were meant to inspire enthusiasm for the war effort, and more like revolutionary political rallies, than victory parties or national holidays. Celebrations were not held in every town—they were held where bands of patriots took the trouble to organize them.

Although it has been suggested, often and pedantically, that the holiday ought to be celebrated on July second, when Congress actually voted for independence, the Declaration itself reads "July Fourth, 1776," and it was the ringing language of Jefferson's Declaration that announced American independence to the people of America and the world. By July of 1777, no one thought to inquire on precisely what day independence had been voted. The Declaration of Independence was dated July fourth; therefore, Independence Day was celebrated on the fourth of July.

A Tradition Emerges

The first anniversary of American Independence was celebrated in only a few towns, but descriptions of those celebrations, printed in newspapers throughout the colonies,[8] were probably instrumental in encouraging others to celebrate the holiday the following year. On June 24, 1778, a committee to plan a Fourth of July celebration was appointed by the Continental Congress in session at York, Pennsylvania, since Philadelphia had passed the winter in British hands. By July, the British Army had moved to New York and Congress was back in Philadelphia. There they celebrated Independence Day with considerable ceremony for a government whose future was very much an open question.

Members of Congress and military officers gathered at City Tavern for a grand dinner replete with 13 set toasts and music, and attended church in a body on Sunday, July 5.[9] Congress' announcement of plans to celebrate Independence Day, together with reports of Independence exercises and banquets held the previous year, made the Fourth of July 1778 a holiday celebrated throughout the colonies.

The Continental Army celebrated the anniversary of American Independence at Brunswick Landing, New Jersey. Double rations of rum were served and General Washington ordered the soldiers to "adorn their hats with green-boughs and to make the best appearance possible"—no easy feat for the rag-tag Continentals. The troops lined up for a full-dress parade and 13 cannon were fired. The entire army then fired three rounds and gave three cheers, each time shouting "Perpetual and undisturbed Independence to the United States of America"—a much larger mouthful than the conventional "hip, hip, hurrah."[10]

Fourth of July celebrations held in 1778, along with the smaller number held the previous year, established an enduring pattern of holiday observance by featuring large amounts of noise. Wherever the holiday was celebrated, church bells rang. Usually the militia paraded, and when they paraded they fired salutes, typically 13 volleys. If the town was fortified or had military ships in its harbor, cannon were fired. At Newport, Rhode Island in 1781, forts guarding the harbor joined ships of the French fleet in firing salutes at sunrise, noon and sunset. The Rhode Island militia hosted French officers at a Fourth of July dinner, and in the evening French sailors on ships in the harbor admired the town, illuminated by hundreds of candles, while citizens of Newport enjoyed the spectacle of sky rockets fired by the fleet in honor of the day.[11] Even towns that lacked forts sometimes possessed cannon; in 1778, Princeton, New Jersey fired rounds with cannon captured from Burgoyne's army. [12]

After the militia parade, government officials, military officers and clergymen, along with other prominent citizens and visitors, attended a dinner held in a large public building.[13] This dinner invariably concluded with 13 patriotic toasts. It was the dinner and accompanying toasts that comprised the core of early Fourth of July celebrations, rapidly becoming so well established that such dinners were held in improbable places.

In 1781, a group of American soldiers held prisoner by the British at Graves End on Long Island assembled under a flag bearing a portrait of General Washington to commemorate the anniversary of "American Independency." Among the 13 toasts they drank was one wishing "a Speedy Releasment to the Allied Prisoners."[14] Fourth of July dinners were also held during the war by American communities in Europe.[15] The day sometimes ended with fireworks, and again the favored number was 13. In Boston in 1779 the display included 13 rockets fired simultaneously, representing the 13 rising states.[16] The number 13 became an early and important symbol of nationhood, since success in the war depended upon the unity of all 13 colonies and that unity was very, very fragile.

If the Fourth of July fell on a Sunday, as it did for the first time in 1779, the celebration was put off until Monday the fifth. Ladies did not attend the dinner in any case; this was the celebration of a political event and politics were of no concern to women. A few women and girls might observe the militia parade from the fringes of the crowd, but public events of this type were all-male affairs.

The citizens of New Haven, Connecticut kept the Sabbath in the Puritan style, from sunset on Saturday until sunset on Sunday. After the Sabbath ended at nightfall on July 4, 1779, there was a meeting at "the old middle brick church," which, like other New England churches, served as a house of worship on Sunday and a civic meeting hall on weekdays. Citizens came to plan ceremonies for the following day, which was expected to be New Haven's first Fourth of July celebration. It was decided that the Second Company of the Governor's Foot Guards would lead a grand procession of citizens and delegations from nearby towns to the Green, where orations would be given.[17] But these fine plans were squelched by British troops.

Daylight on the morning of the fifth revealed a British fleet in the harbor and word quickly spread through town that President Ezra Stiles of Yale, watching with a spyglass from the tower of the college chapel, had seen British troops landing at West Haven. Instead of parading and listening to speeches, the New Haven militia spent two days fighting British regulars, who were harassing the Connecticut coast. They seem to have been attempting to draw Washington from his position at White Plains, opening an opportunity to capture the Hudson Valley and cut New England off from the middle states. Washington stood firm and the British, leaving casualties on both sides, sailed back to New York.[18]

The military parades, dinners and fireworks of 1778, 1779, 1780 and 1781 were not held to celebrate deeds done long ago by men oddly dressed in ponytails and knee britches. They celebrated, as the men of Newbern, North Carolina put it in 1778, "the THIRD year of their INDEPENDENCE, in spite of numerous fleets and armies; in spite of tomahawk and scalping knife; in spite of the numberless wicked and diabolical engines of cruelty and revenge, played off against us by the magnanimous and heroic, humane and merciful George the Third, the father of his people, and his wicked and abandoned soldiery."[19] The satire is heavy handed and the language, as in all revolutionary documents, is exaggerated. George III was no democrat, but neither was he a merciless tyrant, and the British troops were fairly well behaved. But there was a war on and these men were fighting for their lives, their property, and their political rights.

Men who stood to toast Independence in the 1770s knew that they might soon be called upon to fight and die for it. The infamous Wyoming Valley massacre of independence-minded settlers by Indian and Tory troops took place on July 3 and 4, 1778, near Wilkes-Barre, Pennsylvania, and the Fourth of July that same year found George Rogers Clark and his men capturing the British held settlement of Kaskaskia on the Mississippi.

Cannonading salutes, ringing bells, militia drills, dinners and toasts were expressions of revolutionary ardor. Many loyalist or politically apathetic citizens simply stayed at home while the revolutionaries celebrated their holiday. Only with the successful conclusion of the war did the Fourth of July cease to be the annual political rally of a revolutionary party and become the national holiday of a sovereign people.

Notes

1. *Adams Family Correspondence*, L. H. Butterfield, editor, Volume 2, The Belknap Press of Harvard University Press, Cambridge, 1963; Robert Pettus Hay, "Freedom's Jubilee: One Hundred Years of the Fourth of July, 1776–1876," dissertation, University of Kentucky, 1963; *Pennsylvania Gazette*, Philadelphia, July 9, 1777.

2. William Gordon, *The Separation of the Jewish Tribes, after the death of Solomon, accounted for, and applied to the present day, in a sermon preached before the General Court, on Friday, July the Fourth, 1777. Being the Anniversary of the Declaration of Independence.* J. Gill, Boston, 1777.

3. *The Boston Gazette and Country Journal,* July 7, 1777.

4. *Pennsylvania Evening Post,* July 29, 1777. Interestingly, the report is datelined "Portsmouth, July 12," which may indicate that the Portsmouth correspondent did not think the celebration sufficiently newsworthy to write to Philadelphia about until he saw the reports of the Boston celebration in the *Boston Gazette* of July 7.

5. *The Providence Gazette and Country Journal,* July 5, 1777.

6. *The Continental Journal and Weekly Advertiser,* Boston, July 31, 1777; *Pennsylvania Evening Post,* July 29, 1777.

7. James Spear Loring, *The Hundred Boston Orators Appointed by the Municipal Authorities and Other Public Bodies from 1770 to 1852,* John P. Jewett & Co., Boston, 1852.

8. *Virginia Gazette,* July 18, 1777; *Maryland Journal,* July 15, 1777; *Connecticut Gazette,* July 11, 1777.

9. *Pennsylvania Packet,* July 6, 1778; letter from James Lovell to Abigail Adams, 10. July 9, 1778, *Adams Family Correspondence,* Volume III, L.H. Butterfield and Marc Friedlaender, editors, Harvard University Press, 1973; *Pennsylvania Evening Post,* July 8, 1778.

10. "General Orders" for July 3 and July 4, 1778, *The Writings of General Washington from the Original Manuscripts, 1745–1799,* John C. Fitzpatrick, editor, U.S. Government Printing Office, Washington, D.C. 1931–1944, p. 154, Volume 12; entry for July 4, 1778, *Diary of a Common Soldier in the American Revolution 1775–1783; An Annotated Edition of the Journal of Jeremiah Greenman,* edited by Robert C. Bray and Paul E. Bushnell, Northern Illinois University Press, DeKalb, Illinois, 1978; "Journal of Henry Dearborn," *Massachusetts Historical Society Proceedings,* November, 1886, p. 177.

11. *Newport Mercury,* July 7, 1781.

12. *New Jersey Gazette,* July 8, 1778.

13. *Adams Family Correspondence,* L. H. Butterfield and Marc Friedlaender, editors, Harvard University Press, Cambridge, 1973, Mercy Otis Warren to Abigail Adams, July 6, 1779; *Extracts from the Diary of Christopher Marshall, Kept at Philadelphia and Lancaster During the American Revolution, 1774–1781*; William Duane, Joel Munsell, editors 1877, entries for July 5, 1779, July 4, 1780; *Documents Relating to the Revolutionary History of the State of New Jersey, Volume IV–Extracts from*

American Newspapers, William Nelson, editor, State Gazette Publishing Co., Trenton, 1914, pp. 505–507, for accounts of Princeton and Trenton celebrations in 1780; Robert Pettus Hay, "Freedom's Jubilee: One Hundred Years of the Fourth of July, 1776–1876," dissertation, University of Kentucky, Lexington, 1967. The Hay dissertation includes a very complete list of early newspaper accounts of Fourth of July celebrations.

14. *Diary of a Common Soldier in the American Revolution, 1775–1783, An Annotated Edition of the Journal of Jeremiah Greenman*, Robert C. Bray and Paul E. Bushnell, editors, Northern Illinois University Press, De Kalb, 1978, p. 212.

15. "Diary of William Green," for the year 1778, *Massachusetts Historical Society Proceedings*, December, 1920, pp. 128, 129; *Diary of John Quincy Adams*, for 1781, David Grayson Allen, Taylor, Friedlaender, and Walker, editors, p. 88.

16. *Boston Gazette*, July 12, 1779.

17. Charles H. Townshend, *The British Invasion of New Haven, Connecticut*, New Haven, 1879, p. 57.

18. Rollin G. Osterweis, *Three Centuries of New Haven, 1638–1938*, Yale University Press, New Haven, 1953.

19. *The North Carolina Gazette*, New Bern, July 10, 1778.

Constitutional
Contention   3

News of the Treaty of Paris, concluding peace between Britain and an independent United States, reached America in March of 1783. Real problems lay ahead for the young nation, which needed to invent and implement a stable system of national government and to recover from the economic dislocations of war. But all difficulties were overshadowed by the magnificence of the achievement. Americans had won independence from the most powerful empire on earth, and could enjoy their new freedom as citizens of the world's only republic.

Our First National Holiday

Bursting with enthusiasm, patriots prepared to celebrate the first peacetime anniversary of a republic that they proudly compared to ancient Rome.

Everywhere, guns fired 13 volleys and bells rang out—except in Charleston, South Carolina, where all of the town's bells had been taken by the British during the war. Charleston did have a parade of Continental artillery complete with field pieces, a band and flags. The governor gave a dinner at the State House, and there were fireworks in front of the historic Exchange building and a general illumination of the city by candlelight.[1]

Ships in harbors up and down the coast displayed their colors, except as everyone noticed, the British ships. French and Dutch captains were glad to run up their flags, listen to the salutes fired by American ships and watch the fireworks displayed over the harbors. Many towns enjoyed militia parades and dinners for the principal gentlemen with the inevitable 13 patriotic toasts, but Philadelphia procured the most illustrious guest for its celebration. At July Fourth commencement ceremonies at the University of Pennsylvania, George Washington was given the honorary degree of doctor of laws. Philadelphians also watched a parade by 1,500 soldiers whose three-year terms of enlistment in the soon-to-be-disbanded Continental Army had not yet expired.[2]

The war was over but the task of building a nation lay ahead. America needed to create institutions of government, of course, but also a common body of myth and experience that would make the widely scattered citizens of 13 states view themselves as part of a single nation. Our first national holiday, the Fourth of July was an occasion for the fledgling nation to express its unity through the retelling of the heroic struggles of the War of Independence. Many Americans had been less than enthusiastic supporters of the war and most had preferred to tend their farms and shops rather than fight in the ill-paid and poorly equipped army.

During the war, Washington had frequently been reviled as a general who only knew how to retreat. He was accused of being afraid to fight and dismissed as an amateur or a loser. With victory, Washington became a hero in line for rapid promotion to demi-god. There was an outpouring of praise, honors, laudatory odes, editorials, essays, songs and speeches extolling Washington, which reached an annual crescendo on the Fourth of July when poems like this one were distributed as broadsides and published in every newspaper.

Great CINCINNATUS, first and best,
Thy merits ne'er can be expresst,
Though ev'ry muse attends;
'Twas thou alone, divinely taught,
That strangely conquer'd, nobly fought,
Supported by thy friends.[3]

Once independence became a reality, every American seemed transformed into a patriot ready to celebrate the glorious cause. From New England to

Georgia, bells rang, dinners were held, cannons boomed out 13 volleys, and the militia paraded in joyous celebration of Independence.

Prominent among those celebrating the birthday of American Independence were members of the Society of Cincinnati. Named after the famous Roman general who twice left his plow in the fields to save Rome from destruction, and both times returned to his farm once Rome was safe, the society was a patriotic organization formed by officers of the Continental Army before they disbanded in 1783. Membership in the Cincinnati was restricted to officers and their firstborn sons, opening the society to criticism by democrats who accused them of attempting to form an American aristocracy. For many years, the Society of Cincinnati held annual meetings on the Fourth of July in each state capital. After electing officers for the coming year and attending to other organizational business, the members attended public celebrations of the day and held a grand dinner which, naturally, concluded with 13 patriotic toasts.[4]

As the war receded into memory, the Fourth of July lost popularity. A holiday that had been celebrated to promote the cause of independence and then, in 1783, with special enthusiasm as a victory celebration, seemed less important now that independence was secure. Celebrations were fewer and smaller in the years after the war, until the custom was revived as part of a political battle.

Designing a More Perfect Union

Independence was an established fact in the 1780s, but the loose confederation of 13 independent states was not an effective form of government. Congress, under the Articles of Confederation, not only lacked authority to tax and, therefore, had no funds for defense or for projects that would serve the common interest of the states, it lacked authority to regulate interstate commerce. When states squabbled about duties on interstate commerce, fishing rights and passage through territorial waters, there was no higher authority to which to turn for arbitration.

Attention was drawn to the deficiencies of Confederation when farmers in western Massachusetts rebelled against heavy taxes in the fall of 1786. The government of the Commonwealth appealed to the Confederation for help, but the Confederation was impotent. Massachusetts settled the rebellion with very little bloodshed, resolving the underlying problems with some changes in taxation policies and the fortunate return of prosperity following the postwar recession, but the specter of rebellion against a powerless central government haunted the nation.

Many a revolution has won military victory only to fail to create a government capable of ensuring both liberty and domestic tranquility. With a mandate to improve on the government provided by the Articles of Confederation, delegates from 12 states (stubbornly independent Rhode Island refused to participate) assembled in Philadelphia in May 1787 for what would become the Constitutional Convention.

The convention that met in closed sessions in Philadelphia for four hot months in the summer of 1787 was one of the greatest political gatherings in history. Fifty-five men met to design a government for the new nation and although they did not write a perfect document, they did form a more perfect union among the 13 states and establish a very high standard of justice. Domestic tranquility has been seriously disrupted by only one civil war in the two centuries since that summer in Philadelphia, and the constitutional government it created has provided well for the common defense. It has promoted the general welfare to such an extent that the United States is today among the wealthiest nations on earth. The blessings of liberty that were secured by the founders for themselves have been passed down to their posterity.

The Struggle for Ratification

It was, however, not clear to anyone in 1787 that the new Constitution would become a document revered by later generations as a model of excellence in the design of constitutional government. Supporters of the Constitution viewed it as an imperfect document born of compromise, though perhaps the best obtainable given the political realities of the day. Only 39 of the 55 delegates were even willing to sign the Constitution they had written.

The New York delegation, excepting only Alexander Hamilton, withdrew from the convention, leaving a mere 11 states represented when the convention drew to a close in September, inspiring the resourceful Gouverneur Morris to devise wording to make it appear that the states were in agreement: "Done in Convention, by the unanimous consent of the States present the 17 September," which actually meant "done without Rhode Island and New York." The delegates were so certain of meeting opposition from state legislatures that they provided for ratification by specially elected conventions in each state, and so certain that some states would balk altogether that they provided in Article VII for the Constitution to go into effect upon ratification by just nine states.

The Constitution of the United States was drawn up and presented for ratification less than 10 years after the American people had fought a war of independence against a powerful, centralized and distant government—a rebellion incited in large measure by the taxation policies of that government. Yet here was a proposal to create a powerful, central government distant from most of its citizens, in an era of slow travel on bad roads. And the salient argument in favor of the creation of a federal government was the need to raise tax revenues from the citizens of every state. Small wonder that many of the revolutionaries of 1776 rose to object. The debate over ratification of the Constitution was our first national political battle, and it aroused intense feelings on both sides.

Delaware, realizing that the bicameral legislature with two Senate seats for every state gave disproportionate power to small states, became the first state to ratify the Constitution, acting unanimously on December 7, 1787. Pennsylvania Federalists rammed ratification through a hastily elected convention on December 12, 1787, before the Anti-Federalists had time to organize. New Jersey and Georgia, two more small states, ratified unanimously on December 18 and January 2. Federalist Connecticut, one of the larger states in terms of population, ratified on January 9, 1788. Then the going got rough.

Argument and invective flew across newspaper pages and tavern tables as Anti-Federalists accused Federalists of trying to set up a government that would be too strong and would tend toward monarchy. Federalists accused their opponents of being willing to allow the hard-won gains of the Revolution to dissolve in anarchy. Cogent arguments were made both for and against the Constitution, but the most persuasive argument was that America's two most famous and beloved citizens were in favor of ratification: Washington, who sat as president of the Constitutional Convention, and Franklin, who favored the Constitution even though he personally preferred a unicameral legislature.

On the last day of the convention, Franklin rose to give the famous speech on harmony in which he told the delegates, many of whom had seen their preferred forms of government left out of the final document, "The older I grow, the more I am apt to doubt my own judgment." Moreover, Franklin, who had spent much of his adult life in London and Paris, knew that British Tories were waiting to hear that Americans, having fought a successful war, could not form a successful government. Franklin wanted the new nation to be a success. He wanted the Constitution to be ratified, and his opinion weighed heavily in the public mind. Even more importantly, Washington, great Cincinnatus of the War of Independence, supported the Constitution. Despite Franklin's arguments and Washington's support, some delegates went home to lead anti-ratification fights in their state conventions.

The ratification contests in Massachusetts, New Hampshire, Virginia, South Carolina and New York were hard-fought. There was very little debate in Rhode Island, where few supporters of the Constitution could be found. In fact, if Delaware is called the First State, Rhode Island may be designated the Reluctant State, having stubbornly refused to ratify until 1790, when the federal government threatened to cut off trade—and even then ratification passed only by a narrow 34-to-32 vote. Anti-Federalists in Maryland and Massachusetts, where the ratification vote would be very close, insisted that their state conventions propose the addition of a Bill of Rights to the Constitution. Throughout the storm of political controversy, ratification was gaining, state by state. Massachusetts ratified on February 6, Maryland on April 28, South Carolina on May 23, and New Hampshire became the ninth state, putting ratification over the top on June 21, 1788. Yet without Virginia, the new republic could not stand, and the Virginia convention was engaged in a heated ratification debate, with Patrick Henry as the leading speaker for the opposition. When Virginia ratified on June 26, the establishment of the new Constitution was assured. New York ratified on July 26, leaving North Carolina and Rhode Island to straggle in one and two years late.

When news of the New Hampshire and Virginia ratifications reached other states, spontaneous celebrations broke out among Federalists, who rang the church bells and fired nine cannon salutes in honor of the ratifying states.[5] Northern states first heard the news from New Hampshire and Southern states learned first of the Virginia ratification. Joy and the impulse to celebrate were redoubled when it was learned that a 10th state, one more than the required nine, had ratified. Throughout the nation, Federalists agreed that the ratification of the new Constitution, which came only a few days before the anniversary of American independence, should be celebrated on the Fourth of July. Fourth of July celebrations in many New England cities, planned to commemorate the New Hampshire ratification, were interrupted by news of the Virginia ratification, causing the Federalist crowds to cheer wildly.[6]

A Young Republic Celebrates

Sunrise in Philadelphia on July 4, 1788, was greeted by the pealing of bells and the boom of cannon from the ship *Rising Sun*, anchored off Market Street. A brisk wind whipped the hundreds of flags and pennants that festooned the city's streets and wharves. In the harbor a line of 10 ships rode at anchor. From the mast of each ship waved a great white flag on which gold letters spelled out the names of one of the 10 states that had ratified the Constitution. Philadelphia, the city where the Constitution had been written, was ready to celebrate.

In the four days since news of the New Hampshire and Virginia ratifications had reached the city, Philadelphians had been in a frenzy of activity, planning a Grand Federal Procession that assembled at eight o'clock in the morning at the corner of South Street and Third. At 9:30, the parade of 5,000 men moved along Third Street toward Callowhill, led by 12 axmen in white frocks representing pioneers. They were followed by a company of dragoons and after these came John Nixon, the patriot who gave the Declaration its first public reading at the State House in Philadelphia on July 8, 1776. Nixon carried a liberty cap and a flag that read "Fourth of July, 1776." There were more troops, more banners, marching bands and dignitaries, including three justices of the Pennsylvania Supreme Court, who rode in a giant bald eagle, grasping an olive branch and 13 arrows in its talons and pulled by six horses

These were followed by more militia, more notables and more floats, including one drawn by 10 white horses representing the grand federal edifice as a dome supported by 10 columns. But the grandest marchers in the procession were the hundreds upon hundreds of tradesmen who poured through the streets of Philadelphia. First came farmers with plows and oxen, then gunsmiths, goldsmiths, cordwainers, coopers, blacksmiths, whitesmiths, nailers, and staymakers, 77 trades in all, each man carrying the tools of his trade. The manufacturing society had a huge float with carding and spinning machinery, three master weavers at work at various types of looms, and the machine which, in 1773, had been the first in the colonies to print calico patterns on muslin fabric.

In the five days since the news of ratification arrived, the sailors and shipbuilders of Philadelphia had built the ship *Union*, a 33-foot vessel pulled by 10 horses and manned by sailors who climbed the rigging, trimmed her sails to the wind each time the parade rounded a corner and cast anchor at the end of the line of march. Following the tradesmen came more militia units, judges, lawyers, city officials, a rabbi and ministers of several denominations, students with their teachers and professors, and the night watchmen of Philadelphia calling out the hour of ten o'clock on a glorious starlit morning, in cheerful allusion to the 10 ratifying states.

The procession ended on the spacious lawn of William Hamilton, Esq. at Bush Hill, where James Wilson, one of the principal framers of the Constitution, stood to deliver an oration from the domed float that represented the Grand Federal Edifice. The entire company ate dinner on the lawn, followed by 10 patriotic toasts, each toast punctuated by a 10-round artillery salute.[7]

The procession of tradesmen and citizens fit the spirit of the age, emphasizing both the manufacturing and commercial strength of the young nation, and the proud fact that this was a government of the people. A similar trades procession was held in Portsmouth, New Hampshire on June 26 to celebrate the ratification of the Constitution,[8] and the citizens of New Haven, Connecticut celebrated the Fourth of July with a trades procession that featured hundreds of citizens and a float representing the Constitution as a fully rigged ship under full sail, mounting 20 guns and pulled by 10 seamen.[9]

The Constitution was often depicted as an edifice, requiring the support of the states as pillars, or as a ship embarking on a voyage. An earlier but still popular image was of the 13 states as a new constellation in the firmament of nations. These representations were so popular that when the United States built a navy, its great warships were named *Constellation* and *Constitution*. The unifying effect of such symbols was important to the process of making a nation out of a collection of newly independent colonies.

South Carolina and Georgia did not learn of the New Hampshire and Virginia ratifications until after the Fourth of July. Federalists in other towns, like Groton, Massachusetts, had not heard the news from Virginia, but joyfully celebrated the ratification by a ninth state, New Hampshire. The citizens of Groton erected nine pillars on the town common and fired nine volleys, which surprised many who recalled that only five months earlier Groton had instructed its representative to the state convention to vote against ratification.[10]

Some men who had opposed the Constitution became caught up in the general enthusiasm once ratification was assured; but Anti-Federalist strongholds such as Norton, Massachusetts, fired the traditional 13 salutes, not the Federalist nine.[11] And at Georgetown, in that part of Virginia that would become Kentucky, pioneers who felt neglected by their parent colony of Virginia drank 14 toasts and fired 14 rifles, for each of the original 13 states and for the 14th state that they hoped soon to become.[12]

Carlisle, Pennsylvania was typical in the division of opinion that its celebration exhibited. The militia assembled in the public square at 10 in the morning to see Mr. Michael Ege present the Federal Society with a cannon recently cast at his furnace and emblazoned with the word Federal. After listening to an oration at the Presbyterian Church, the Federalists had dinner at Letart Springs, where they heard 10 toasts, each accompanied by a discharge from the new federal artillery piece. A separate, anti-ratification group repaired to dine at Meeting House Springs, where they heard 13 toasts, including one to "the virtuous minority of the late convention of Philadelphia," which is to say, those who had opposed the Constitution, preferring merely to amend the Articles of Confederation.[13] Since Pennsylvania had already ratified the Constitution, the resentful toasts of Anti-Federalists had little immediate political importance, but in New York and Rhode Island, ratification was an open political question.

At Albany, where news of the Virginia ratification arrived on July 3, Federalists and Anti-Federalists agreed to hold a joint celebration at which 13 cannon and 13 rounds of musketry would be fired; the two parties would dine separately. Despite this agreement, on the morning of the fourth, the Anti-Federalists marched to the edge of town, where they fired 13 salutes and burned a copy of the new Constitution. This was too much for the Federalists to stomach; after dinner they marched, 800 to 1,000 strong, to the spot where the Constitution had been burned, planted a Liberty tree and fired 10 salutes. Upon their return to town, the Federalists were confronted in Green Street by anti-Constitution men armed with clubs, stones and a field-piece. The melee lasted 20 minutes, leaving the Federalists victorious, several participants wounded and one dead.[14]

Rhode Island narrowly escaped a similarly bloody confrontation. When news of the New Hampshire ratification reached Providence on June 24, bells rang out and the city's intrepid Federalists, few in number in a state that had refused so much as to send a delegate to the Constitutional Convention, planned a Fourth of July celebration on private property north of the city. A general invitation was issued and an ox was set to roasting through the night of July third. During the evening, Anti-Federalist farmers, carrying muskets and intent on stopping the Federalist celebration, assembled in the woods near the picnic site. It is impossible, 200 years later, to ascertain the number of these angry farmers. Federalists at the time claimed that there were a mere 300; Anti-Federalists boasted that there were 1,000, with 2,000 more on the way. The battle never took place. Shortly after sunrise, a delegation of frightened and outnumbered Federalists met with the angry farmers and agreed that the celebration would honor the Fourth of July—not the Constitution; that there would be 13 salutes—not nine; and that there would be no toasts in honor of the nine ratifying states. Having won their point, the soldiers of Anti-Federalism went peaceably home,[15] but the clash between pro- and anti-Constitution men in 1788 foreshadowed the two-party system that would soon come to dominate American politics.

Notes

1.   *South Carolina Gazette and the General Advertiser*, July 5, 1783.
2.   *Freeman's Journal or North American Intelligencer*, July 9, 1783; Greenman, *Diary of a Common Soldier*, p. 237; Adelaide L. Fries, "An Early Fourth of July Celebration," *Journal of American History*, Summer 1915, pp. 469–474, and Hay, *Freedom's Jubilee*.
3.   *Daily Advertiser* (New York), July 4, 1786.
4.   *The Gazette of the State of Georgia* (Savannah), July 8, 1784; *The Newport Mercury* (Rhode Island), July 10, 1784, July 9, 1785; *The Independent Gazetteer or the Chronicle of Freedom* (Philadelphia), July 9, 1785; *The Pennsylvania Mercury and Universal Advertiser* (Philadelphia), July 8, 1785; *The American Mercury* (Hartford), July 11, 1785; *The Daily Advertiser* (New York), July 4, 1786, July 5, 1786; *American Herald* (Boston), July 11, 1785; *New Hampshire Spy* (Portsmouth), July 7, 1787; *The Georgia Gazette or Independent Register* (Augusta), July 14, 1787; *The South Carolina Gazette and General Advertiser*, July 6, 1784; *Columbian Herald* (Charleston), July 4 and 6, 1785; *Connecticut Courant* July 11, 1785.

5. *Boston Gazette*, June 30, 1788; *Newport Mercury*, July 9, 1788; *Connecticut Gazette*, July 11, 1788; *Independent Chronicle* (of Boston), June 26, 1788; *Maryland Journal and Baltimore Advertiser*, July 15, 1788.

6. *Connecticut Courant*, July 7, 1788; *Boston Gazette*, July 7, 1788; *Diary of John Quincy Adams*, for July 4, 1788, David Grayson Allen, Taylor, Friedlaender and Walker, editors, Harvard University Press, Cambridge, 1981; *Independent Chronicle* (of Boston), July 10, 1788.

7. *A Brief History of the Revolution with a Sketch of the Life of Captain John Hewson*, Philadelphia, 1843; *Independent Gazette or Chronicle of Freedom* (Philadelphia), July 4, 1788; *Pennsylvania Packet* (Philadelphia), July 4, 1788.

8. *Boston Gazette*, June 30, 1788.

9. *Connecticut Courant*, July 14, 1788.

10. *Independent Chronicle* (of Boston), July 10, 1788.

11. *Independent Chronicle* (of Boston), July 10, 1788.

12. *Kentucke Gazette*, July 5, 1788; Robert Pettus Hay, "A Jubilee for Freemen: The Fourth of July on Frontier Kentucky, 1788–1816," *The Register of the Kentucky Historical Society*, July 1966.

13. *Carlisle Gazette*, July 9, 1788.

14. *Connecticut Courant*, July 14, 1788; *Daily Advertiser* (New York), July 10, 1788.

15. *Newport Mercury*, July 9, 1788; *United States Chronicle* (of Providence), July 3, 10, 1788.

Political
Fireworks 4

Political controversy crystallized into two political parties around the personalities of Thomas Jefferson and Alexander Hamilton.

Thomas Jefferson, the Virginia aristocrat, cherished a vision of America as an agrarian democracy designed to ensure liberty to each individual. When he returned to Virginia in 1789 from Paris, where he had served the United States as minister to France, his sympathies were with the revolutionaries who had overthrown the king.

The illegitimate son of upper-class West Indian parents, Alexander Hamilton was a self-made man, an outstanding young officer on Washington's staff during the war and a brilliant lawyer with a masterful command of the intricacies of finance in a generation when the subject was understood by few statesmen—not including Jefferson. Hamilton served as Washington's secretary of the treasury, put the new nation on sound financial footing and became Jefferson's political nemesis. Hamilton always feared the rule of a revolutionary mob. He believed that democracy could succeed only under the direction of a governing elite and that America needed to become a nation of manufacturers and merchants.

News of the Revolution in France, beginning with the fall of the Bastille on July 14, 1789, was at first greeted with nearly universal enthusiasm in America. Indeed, when Fourth of July festivities were rained out in Philadelphia in 1792, the celebration was postponed until Bastille Day, July 14.[1] By 1793, news of the guillotining of Louis XVI, friend of our own Revolution, rumors of rampant atheism and the beginnings of the Reign of Terror cooled the ardor of many more conservative—which is to say Federalist—Americans for the French Revolution, and heated up the contention between Jeffersonian Democratic-Republicans and Hamiltonian Federalists.

Partisan Squabbles

Rarely before or since have American politics descended to the depths of bitter partisan contention that they reached as the 19th century began. Jefferson and his party were widely believed to be atheists bent on leading the country into a disastrous repetition of the French Revolution, while President John Adams was regarded as an autocrat who, with his Federalist friends, favored British-style monarchy over democratic institutions. The republic was too young to regard political arguments over foreign and domestic policy with equanimity, and many feared that the election results could condemn the country to the turmoil of political revolution—or send it back into the arms of Great Britain.

Political campaigns in this highly charged partisan atmosphere were nasty affairs, with false and scurrilous charges flung by both sides. A time of intense political rivalry, such epithets as "French agent," "tyrant," "monarchist" and "atheist" were routinely flung at presidential candidates. And the epithet "dangerous man" offered by Alexander Hamilton was enough to cost Aaron Burr the election for governor of New York. Hamilton had stood by his characterization of Burr and went to Weehawken Heights that morning in 1804 determined to defend his honor against a man whom, along with President Jefferson and his administration, Hamilton believed capable of plunging America into Jacobin anarchy. Hamilton's death in the duel ended Burr's career and removed two leading figures from the American political scene. Strife between the two parties continued.

Partisan feeling ran so high that in many towns supporters of the rival parties could not agree to sit down together at dinner on the Fourth of July. Two complete and separate celebrations had to be planned, oneE for Federalists and one for Democratic-Republicans—although in towns like Newburyport, Massachusetts, where there were precious few Jeffersonian Democrats, or Frankfort, Kentucky, where Federalists were scarce, a single celebration sufficed.[2] Indeed, when the men of Hagers-Town, Maryland agreed to have "gentlemen of different political parties" participate in the same exercises in 1812, they were so proud of themselves that they boasted about it in the newspaper.[3]

Patterns of Celebration

There was no government bureau to mandate or standardize Fourth of July exercises. Celebrations depended on the initiative of citizens who formed committees to sponsor and pay for whatever festivity they thought appropriate or could afford. When no one stepped forward to organize an official ceremony, the town had none.[4]

But the Fourth of July was an important holiday in a society that had relatively few holidays. There was Election Day, on dates that varied from town to town even for presidential elections, and Muster Day, when all able-bodied men of military age turned out to drill in the militia—although Muster Day was passing into history in the more established regions, where fear of Indian attack was a memory from the distant past. New England celebrated Thanksgiving[5] and the rest of the nation celebrated Christmas. Many larger towns held some sort of observance of Washington's birthday. But the Fourth of July was the only national holiday, and few towns let it pass without some official recognition.

Throughout the nation, the Fourth of July was ushered in with the ringing of bells and the boom of cannon. Towns arranged for the bells of every church and public building to be rung for a specified period, usually 15 minutes or half an hour, following sunrise. If the town had cannon, these were fired at sunrise in a National Salute, one volley for each of the 15 states; Vermont and Kentucky joined the Union in 1791 and 1792. Often, bells would ring and cannon boom again at noon and at sunset.

The typical program for Fourth of July exercises was patterned on the familiar proceedings of church services and Muster Day. Nothing could seem more appropriate to a nation newly born in a hard-fought war of independence than for the militia to drill on Independence Day as they did on Muster Day. The little town of Lyme, Connecticut thriftily consolidated two holidays by holding the annual militia drill and election of a new militia captain on July Fourth.[6]

A militia drill was a lively public event. Most of the men and all of the boys in town turned out to watch, and many of the women and girls watched as well. At the edges of the crowd, vendors sold candy, lemonade, gingerbread, and such exotic fruits as dates, figs and limes that could be sucked through a peppermint stick. The militia was well supplied with ale, hard cider and rum to quench the thirst they worked up parading in the hot July sun. The end of the militia drill was marked by a 15-round salute fired with muskets, or cannon, if the local militia boasted an artillery company.

In many towns, the militia drill was followed by a procession and formal patriotic exercises. The militia escorted the governor, mayor, visiting dignitaries, members of the Society of Cincinnati or simply the gentlemen of the place to a large public hall, which, given the general lack of other large public buildings, usually turned out to be a church. Inside the church, the men were carefully seated, with the most eminent gentlemen given the best seats and the Cincinnati seated as a group in a place of honor.

The formal exercises were arranged in a semblance of a Protestant church service, the formal occasion most familiar to Americans of that era. There might be an introductory prayer by a local clergyman, a patriotic song and the reading of a patriotic ode, often written for the occasion by a local poet. Over the years, a reading of the Declaration of Independence was added to the program, especially in areas where the Jeffersonian Democratic-Republicans became dominant. The heart of the program was an oration by a minister, politician or other local notable. Another patriotic song and a benediction by a minister concluded the exercises.

Then the assembly rose and marched from the building in formal procession to a public dinner. The dinner, considered central to the day's proceedings, was held in many towns where there was no formal oration or reading of the Declaration.[7]

Dinner for such a large party was prepared by a local tavern keeper and generally served on a lawn or under a grove of trees, although citizens of larger towns might be able to dine in a large tavern or public building, especially the state houses of capital cities. At the dinner, as at the exercises in the church, men were seated in order of precedence, with the most important at the head table.

All the gentlemen were hot and thirsty, and spirits flowed freely. The 18th century was innocent of the notion of temperance. Ministers, merchants and statesmen lifted a cup as readily as the young farmers and journeymen who had drilled with the militia. It was not uncommon for an oration to be given at the dinner in addition to the one already delivered in the church, but the climax of the meal was toasting. Thirteen or 15 toasts had been arranged earlier in the week, and as the meal ended, prominent citizens rose in turn to give each toast.

There were the inevitable toasts to Washington and to Independence, but others varied with current events. Many diners in 1789 saw fit to toast "the principle of patriotism, and the spirit of union, to pervade the states of North Carolina and Rhode Island," which had not yet ratified the Constitution.[8] In the early years, it was common to toast the King of France, but euphoria over

France's apparently democratic revolution led to a universal toasting of the French Republic. These "set" toasts were followed by "volunteers," or spontaneous toasts, of which there might be as many as 30 or 40, all drunk with prodigious quantities of ale, cider, wine, rum or whiskey. The celebration broke up toward evening and men staggered home to sleep it off.[9]

While there was plenty of space for all who desired to witness the militia drill, large towns had no church able to accommodate the crowds of men who wished to attend the formal exercises, and the even larger crowds eager to attend the public dinner could not be accommodated by a single tavern keeper. Quite sensibly, the problem was solved by holding several exercises, each with its own orator, followed by multiple dinners. In Boston in 1789, the militia drill was curtailed by rain. Nevertheless, the militia escorted state officials, except for the governor, who was ill, to the Stone Chapel, while the Society of Cincinnati walked in procession to the Old Brick Meeting House. The Cincinnati then dined at the Bunch of Grapes Tavern; the Cadets dined at the American Coffee House; the Infantry dined at Hoyt's Hall; and dinner for the Fusiliers was held at the Eastern Coffee House. In an ordinary year, the governor hosted a dinner as well.[10]

The custom of hearing an oration and attending a dinner at which patriotic toasts were offered readily lent itself to the needs of the rapidly developing political parties of the era. With the precedent of multiple orations and dinners already established on grounds of expedience, nothing could be more natural than to add additional orations with a speaker guaranteed to express the sentiments of a particular party, and to arrange Fourth of July dinners at which all of the toasts would be in honor of Jefferson and Democratic-Republican principles, or all in support of Adams, Hamilton and Federalism.

In the years immediately following ratification of the Constitution, most Fourth of July celebrations displayed a distinctly Federalist flavor. Federalism, which triumphed in the ratification contest, was unmistakably the political creed of the hour. Most clergymen, a group frequently chosen as Fourth of July orators, were Federalist, as were the members of the Society of Cincinnati, who took a leading role in early Fourth of July celebrations. Unwilling to see their national holiday become a festival of Federalism, Americans with Anti-Federalist, or Democratic-Republican, sympathies organized orations and dinners of their own.

In New York, the Tammany Society, a patriotic organization founded in support of Democratic principles and formally known as the Columbian Order, held a Fourth of July celebration in 1791 similar to the Federalist-dominated celebrations held in New York and other cities in every way except for the content of the oration and toasts. The Tammany Society, named for the Delaware Chief Tamanend who concluded a treaty with William Penn, was comprised of 13 "tribes" and incorporated many Indian titles and ceremonials

The Tammany Society Fourth of July celebration in 1812, as the procession passes in front of the Wigwam. Some Society members are dressed in ceremonial garb as Indians, others fire guns into the air in celebration. A boy at the right is preparing to fire a toy cannon. (Painting by W. P. Chappel, courtesy of the New-York Historical Society)

into its proceedings. At nine o'clock in the morning members marched in formal procession with a military escort from the Wigwam in Broad Street to the New Dutch Church, where the Grand Sachem read the Declaration of Independence and the Reverend Dr. Linn spoke. After the exercises, the procession marched to the Battery to witness the firing of a federal salute. The Wigwam was illuminated in the evening.[11]

Ladies were invited to attend the exercises in some towns, with the proviso that they must arrive early and seat themselves along the sides of the church and in the gallery so as to be out of the way of the gentlemen when the procession marched grandly in.[12] In exercises held by Federalists, the assemblage would hear an oration on the exemplary character of Washington and the glories of the Constitution; in exercises sponsored by Democratic-Republicans, the crowd would hear about the exemplary character of Washington and the glories of the Declaration of Independence and the Bill of Rights. Either way, a man could leave the church feeling smugly confident of the soundness of his political convictions.

When a Committee on Arrangements was formed, it had the privilege of drawing up the program. If the Federalists formed a committee and the Democrats did not, the latter might grumble, but they could hardly expect the Federalists to select a speaker to suit their taste. Even the Declaration of Independence and the Constitution were dragged into the partisan quarrels. Readings of the Declaration of Independence were extremely popular with Democratic-Republicans, while some Federalists refused to read the document at their celebrations.[13] In Raleigh, North Carolina, where the Declaration was read on the Fourth of July, Joseph Gales, editor of the Democratic *Register*, toasted Jefferson at the Fourth of July dinner as "the sage and patriotic editor of the Declaration of Independence," whereupon William Boylan, editor of the Federalist Raleigh *Minerva*, corrected him, pointing out that Federalist John Adams was a member of the committee that wrote the Declaration and contending that he ought to be given equal credit. The argument ended in a fistfight in which Gales was severely beaten.[14]

Democratic or Federalist, the toasts were usually punctuated with musket or cannon salutes and quite often each toast was followed by a patriotic or political song. Special songs, such as "Adams and Liberty" ("Her pride is her Adams—his laws are her choice") were composed by party loyalists to enliven these political dinners with expressions of proper partisan sentiment. And new lyrics were written to such perennially popular tunes as "Yankey Doodle" to fit the political moment:

> Should Great Britain, Spain or France
> Wage war upon our shore, sir,
> We'll lead them such a woundy dance
> They'll find their toes are sore, sir.

Philadelphians celebrate the Fourth of July, 1812, in Centre Square. (Painting by John Lewis Krimmel, courtesy of the Pennsylvania Academy of Fine Arts)

This painting of the Fourth of July in Philadelphia in 1819 captures the spirit of riotous celebration. Military units parade while boys fire pistols and toy cannon. Two handsome young soldiers celebrate victory as an ancient veteran to their left displays an old war wound. Two young couples sing patriotic ballads they have just purchased from a vendor; an officer offers a toast to a group of enthusiastic dinner companions; a bare-knuckle boxing match begins; and in every corner Americans can be seen saluting the holiday with strong drink. (By John Lewis Krimmel, courtesy of the Historical Society of Pennsylvania)

A "Song on the Non-Importation Act" of 1806 accurately reflects the attitude of the Federalist Northeast toward Jeffersonian foreign policy.

> The motley band of demagogues, who rule our potent nation,
> Have lately put a stop, it seems, to British importation . . .
> Farewell! alas! a long farewell to sparkling old Madeira
> No longer sipped in English glass by this unhappy era
> Our democratic grog must now be drank in German tumblers
> Thick as the heads, coarse as the minds of Democratic bunglers.[15]

Toasts were as partisan as the rest of the celebration. The Federalists of Springfield, Massachusetts "honored" Thomas Jefferson in 1808 with a toast to "The President of the United States—to ruin a country, govern it by a French Philosopher—we hail the fourth of March 1809," when a new President would be inaugurated. The Democratic-Republicans of Kentucky were equally gracious, "honoring" former president John Adams in 1803 with these words: "John Adams' administration is fallen—May it fall like Lucifer, never to rise again."[16]

Fireworks

Not all of the fireworks were contained in incendiary toasts. Increasingly, they were to be found in the sky. Some forms of fireworks, particularly rockets fired by military ships, were part of early Fourth of July celebrations, but fireworks were expensive and America was not born rich.

John Adams' famous letter of July 2, 1776, predicting that the holiday would be "celebrated . . . as the great anniversary festival . . . with bonfires, and illuminations . . ." referred not to fireworks but to the quaint custom of illuminating buildings and public plazas by placing candles in windows or even atop walls and along public ways. The effect was dramatic and made a great impression in the days before streetlights. When a city was dark after sunset every other night in the year, a festive illumination became a memorable event.

Fireworks have been known since ancient times, but they are rarely mentioned in connection with 18th-century Fourth of July celebrations. Although a degree of technical expertise is essential in the preparation of fireworks, instruction was available in books printed in England, and Americans who desired to set off fireworks could have done so. A more convincing explanation for the absence of fireworks from early celebrations is that they were expensive and required advance planning, while early Fourth of July celebrations were simple affairs with more emphasis on politics than on panoply.

A patriotic society, possibly the Society of Cincinnati, parades past Independence Hall with banners flying. (Ink and watercolor by John Lewis Krimmel, courtesy of the Springfield Art Museum, Springfield, Missouri)

Fireworks began to appear with increasing frequency in the first decade of the 19th century. Boston had its first Fourth of July fireworks in 1805, and they were as political as the rest of the day's conspicuously Federalist celebration. From a stage erected for the purpose in the center of the Common, Bostonians were treated to figures representing Justice and Liberty, while busts of Washington and Hamilton were emblazoned in fireworks on the night sky.[17]

Expansionist Sentiments

Political division increased as the United States moved toward the war with Great Britain that began in 1812. Although the rights of Yankee sailors were being violated on the high seas by both British and French navies as those two nations continued their war on the continent, the Federalist seaports and the Northeast in general wanted to settle American differences with England at the negotiating table. The South and, more particularly, the western states from Vermont to Tennessee were eager for a war that would win Florida, Canada and the Northwest for the United States, and allow expansion of the frontier on a grand scale. An exuberant frontiersman raised his cup in Lexington, Kentucky in 1810 to propose a Fourth of July toast to: "The starry flag of Columbia—Before the next anniversary of Independence, may it float triumphant on the ramparts of Quebeck." In New Bedford, Massachusetts sentiments were precisely the opposite. Citizens gathered for a Fourth of July dinner at Caldwell's Hotel in 1811 passed a resolution enumerating no fewer than 57 ways in which conflict with England would be "ruinous to our republic."[18]

On the frontier, where the nearest Federalist was likely to be hundreds of miles away on the other side of the Alleghenies, the Fourth of July was a celebration of American nationalism—and western nationalism was expansionist.

Americans who settled beyond the national borders in territories belonging to the French, Spanish or English often celebrated the Fourth as a provocative expression of the hope that these territories would soon become American. This was true in Natchez in 1797, where the Fourth was celebrated "by all who were hostile to the Spanish government."[19] When Jay's treaty secured the evacuation of British garrisons from the Northwest Territories in 1796, soldiers serving in the first American garrisons celebrated the Fourth of July with extra whiskey rations, the firing of salutes and a day off from work.[20] Conversely, after Wisconsin became part of American territory, the French citizens of Prairie du Chien sullenly refused to celebrate the holiday.[21]

American merchants began to settle in the Sandwich Islands in the 1790s, and while many hoped only to make a profit and sail home, others soon began to dream of annexing the tropical paradise to their beloved republic. The Fourth of July, 1814, was celebrated in the islands that would one day become the 50th state with salutes from ships in the harbor at Honolulu, and a formal dinner at which the American community hosted King Kamehameha. Fourth of July dinners soon became an annual event in Hawaii. By the 1840s, the Fourth of July was celebrated assiduously by an American community, which marked its growing hope of achieving formal political domination of Hawaii with elaborate Fourth of July celebrations. Businesses were closed, children set off firecrackers, salutes honoring American Independence were fired by the Hawaiian government and many Hawaiian chiefs attended dinners in honor of the day.[22]

The Oregon country was for several decades held in an ill-defined joint dominion by the United States and Great Britain, but in the early 1840s a growing stream of American settlers were pushing west and pushing also to make the Northwest American. Settlers in Oregon, who knew that the two governments were negotiating, expressed their hopes for British cession with a lively celebration of Independence Day 1846.[23]

Many Americans assumed that it was America's destiny to displace Great Britain throughout the North American continent, with Canada eventually becoming part of the United States. A considerable number of American farmers seeking land and opportunity settled in the area around York (modern Toronto) in the early 19th century, hoping that the territory would soon become part of the United States. On the Fourth of July, 1817, a group of young men demonstrated their expansionist desires by impudently riding through the streets of town carrying the American flag. Independence Day salutes fired from the guns at Fort Niagara could be heard in the distance. The demonstration did not please the Canadians, who vividly remembered the American sack of their town during the War of 1812.[24]

Not all dreams of American expansion were fulfilled, but Americans were ready to celebrate Independence Day in whatever corner of the globe they found themselves on the Fourth of July. In 1789, a Boston ship, the Columbia Rediviva, was in Nootka Sound, along the shore of Vancouver Island, British Columbia, a remote spot where a clash between two great empires was about to occur.

Both Britain and Spain claimed the area and both, along with Yankee traders, coveted the rich furs that the region offered. Spain and England had each sent ships and men to build trading posts at Nootka. Early in July, the Spanish captured the British crew, and men from all three nations waited tensely for the inevitable British response. At sunrise on Saturday morning startled sailors awakened to the boom of cannon, assuming that a battle had begun. It was only Americans celebrating the Fourth of July.

Like Americans up and down the Atlantic coast, the men aboard the Columbia celebrated with a formal dinner. They invited the imprisoned

British officers and the officers and priests from the Spanish ships and fort to an American-style meal, complete with an exchange of toasts. After dinner, a 13-gun salute from the *Columbia* was answered by thirteen gun salutes from the ship *San Carlos* and from the newly built Fort Miguel.[25]

Yankee crews on long trading or whaling voyages customarily celebrated the Fourth of July, especially when two or more American ships happened to be in the same remote port on Independence Day. Salutes were fired from the ships' guns, the men were given extra rations of rum and, when it was practical, captains gave their crew a holiday and sometimes even went ashore to roast fresh meat and enjoy a real holiday dinner. The journal of Captain Ingraham, Master of the ship *Hope* out of Boston buying furs from Pacific Northwest Indians to sell in China, reveals that on the Fourth of July 1791, he "caused a Hog of 70 lbs. weight to be roasted whole on which we all dined ashore. I with my officers and seamen drank the president's health and made the forest ring with three cheers." However, demonstrating the Yankee industriousness that made America rich, Ingraham continues, "After which every one return'd to their several employments as we could not spare time to set longer after dinner."[26]

Notes

1. *National Gazette*, Philadelphia, July 7, 1792.
2. *Newburyport Herald* for the decade after 1800 for accounts of the Federalist Fourth of July celebrations; Kentucky celebrations are described in Robert Pettus Hay, "A Jubilee for Freemen: The Fourth of July in Frontier Kentucky, 1788–1816," Register of the Kentucky Historical Society, July, 1966, pp. 169–195.
3. *Hagers-Town Gazette* (Maryland), July 7, 1812.
4. *The Diary of William Bentley, D.D.*, published by Peter Smith, Gloucester, Mass., 1962, chronicles the irregular nature of Fourth of July celebrations in Salem, Mass. from 1792–1819.
5. Diana Karter Appelbaum, *Thanksgiving: An American Holiday, An American History*, Facts On File, New York, 1984.
6. *Connecticut Gazette* (New London), July 10, 1799.

7.   Among the sources consulted on the period from the turn of the century to the War of 1812 are: "Private Journals of Mr. John P. Brace," found in Emily Noyes Vanderpoel, *More Chronicles of a Pioneer School from 1792–1833 being added History on the Litchfield Female Academy*, Cadmus Book Shop, New York, 1927; John Marsh, *Travels Through the United States in the Years 1806 & 1807, and 1809, 1810, & 1811*, George Cowie and Co., London 1818, for an account of Louisville, Georgia in 1806; and among the newspapers consulted and not noted elsewhere: *Farmer's Repository* (Charlestown, West Va.); *The Sun* (Pittsfield, Mass.); *Alexandria Gazette* (Va.); *Eastern Argus* (Portland, Maine).

8.   *The Augusta Chronicle and Gazette of the State* (Georgia), July 11, 1789.

9.   For accounts of Fourth of July celebrations in the 1790s, I have drawn on: Robert Pettus Hay, *Freedom's Jubilee*, and "A Jubilee for Freemen: The Fourth of July in Frontier Kentucky, 1788–1816," *The Register of the Kentucky Historical Society*, July, 1966; Fletcher M. Green, "Listen to the Eagle Scream: One Hundred Years of the Fourth of July in North Carolina (1776–1876)," *The North Carolina Historical Review*, July 1954; *The Diary of William Bentley, D.D.*, Peter Smith, Gloucester, Mass., 1962; *Diary of William Dunlap, 1766–1839*, Benjamin Bloom, New York, 1969; and among the many newspapers examined for the period from 1789 to 1799 were *The Newport Mercury*, *The Baltimore Daily Intelligencer*, *The Federal Gazette and Philadelphia Evening Post*, *The Federal Gazette and Daily Advertiser* (New York), *The Connecticut Gazette* (Hartford), *The Boston Gazette and Country Journal*, *The Virginia Gazette and General Advertiser* (Richmond), *The Columbian Mirror and Alexandria Advertiser* (Virginia). Fourth of July stories appear in issues published shortly after July Fourth. Announcements of Fourth of July activities such as the meetings of the Society of Cincinnati appear in the issue immediately preceding July Fourth. July Fourth was a printer's holiday, so that even the daily papers did not appear on July fifth.

10. *Boston Gazette and Country Journal*, July 6, 1789.

11. *The Federal Gazette and Daily Advertiser* (New York), July 6, 1791.

12. *Newport Mercury*, July 7, 1810, and July 4, 1812.

13. Charles Warren, *Jacobin and Junto*, Harvard University Press, Cambridge, 1931, footnote on page 185.

14. Fletcher M. Green, "Listen to the Eagle Scream: One Hundred Years of the Fourth of July in North Carolina," *The North Carolina Historical Review*, July 1954, p. 304.

15. "The Patriotic Vocalist or Fourth of July Pocket Book," Cushing and Appleton, Salem, Mass., 1812 (Shaw-Shoemaker #26390).

16. *Hampshire Federalist*, July 7, 1808; Hay, "Jubilee for Freemen," p. 184.

17. *Newburyport Herald* (Massachusetts), July 6, 1810; *Hampshire Federalist* (Springfield, Mass.), July 7, 1808; *Boston Gazette*, July 8, 1805, July 7, 1806; Remington, "Fourths of the Past," mentions fireworks in New Bedford in 1809.

18. Hay, "Jubilee for Freemen," p. 190; Walter H. B. Remington, "Fourths of the Past," Old Dartmouth Historical Society Sketches, Number 140, Proceedings of the Meeting of the Old Dartmouth Historical Society held June 17, 1914.

19. Francis Bailey, *Journal of a Tour in the Unsettled Parts of America in 1796 and 1797,* Southern Illinois University Press, Carbondale, 1969, entry for July 4, 1797.

20. F. Cleaver Bald, *Detroit's First American Decade, 1796–1805*, University of Michigan Press, Ann Arbor, 1948.

21. "A Journal of Life in Wisconsin 100 Years Ago," kept by Williard Keyes of Newfane, Vermont, *Wisconsin Magazine of History*, June, 1920, p. 443.

22. Harold Whitman Bradley, *The American Frontier in Hawaii; The Pioneers, 1789–1843*, Stanford University Press, California, 1942, pp. 94–95, 118, 267–268.

23. George W. Soliday, "Independence Day in the Far Northwest," *The Washington Historical Quarterly*, July 1913, pp. 178–9.

24. "A Journal of Life in Wisconsin 100 Years Ago," Kept by Williard Keyes of Newfane, Vermont, *Wisconsin Magazine of History*, March, 1920, p. 343.

25. Dagny B. Hanson, "July Fourth, 1789," *American West*, Volume 13, number 4, 1976, pp. 32–34; and O.B. Sperlin, "Earliest Celebrations of Independence Day in the Northwest," *Pacific Northwest Quarterly*, July 1944, pp. 215–222.

26. George W. Soliday, "Independence Day in the Far Northwest," *The Washington Historical Quarterly*, July, 1913.

Freedom's Jubilee   5

The celebration of economic growth and of industry was a new note at patriotic gatherings of the 1820s. Progress would be the theme of the age just beginning, progress visible in the numerous canals being built across the land.

A Groundbreaking Holiday

Ground was broken for the Erie Canal, the first to be built in America, at a ceremony held on the Fourth of July, 1817, near Rome, New York.[1] The Erie Canal opened a new era of transportation in 1825; soon it seemed that canals were being built everywhere, as inland districts strove to share in the prosperity that cheap water transportation made possible.

The Fourth of July in Cleveland in 1827 was turned into a celebration of the opening of the new Ohio Canal with Governor Trimble arriving in Cleveland aboard the first boat, the *State of Ohio*.[2] Cleveland's Fourth of July procession formed at the dock where the governor disembarked and marched to the Public Square for formal exercises.

It was more practical to plan to break ground for a new canal on July Fourth than to expect to finish one just in time for the holiday, and Fourth of July ceremonies held to mark the beginning of new canals became a standard feature of the era. Work on the Ohio Canal had officially begun on July 4, 1825, when Governor DeWitt Clinton of New York, whose state built the first American canal, gave the Fourth of July oration. That same year Governor Oliver Wolcott of Connecticut gave the Fourth of July oration at Granby, Connecticut, marking the start of work on the Farmington Canal. President John Quincy Adams spoke on July 4, 1828, at ceremonies marking the commencement of work on the Chesapeake and Ohio Canal.[3]

Year by year the holiday had grown until by the 1820s it was difficult to find a town where it was not celebrated. So prevalent was the custom of celebrating the Fourth, that when no celebration had been arranged, men would turn out on the Fourth and get up an impromptu celebration with many of the trappings familiar in communities that had planned their ceremonies carefully in advance.[4] These impromptu celebrations captured the essential program of firing salutes, gathering formally to hear the day honored and feasting that was observed throughout the nation.

Patriots Remembered

Most towns planned their Fourth of July celebrations in advance, carefully selecting distinguished citizens to serve as Reader of the Declaration of Independence and Orator of the Day. The Orator, who in the early years of the republic had commonly been a clergyman, was now most frequently a prominent local attorney, often with political ambitions—although larger towns strove to find orators of national stature. The Reader of the Declaration would likewise be a respected local citizen. Since he did not have to be a powerful speaker, like the Orator who was expected to hold the attention of an audience of hundreds for an hour or longer, the pool of potential readers was larger and the choice often fell on an elderly patriot who had participated in the struggle for independence.

Eighty-year-old Col. John Franklin was serving as official Reader during Fourth of July exercises in Bradford County, Pennsylvania in 1828 when he gratified the crowd by following the reading with a spontaneous speech:

Friends and fellow citizens: You see before you a frail remnant of one of those who faced the British cannon, and heard the still more appalling yell of the painted savage of the terrible massacre of Wyoming. We gained for you the liberty you have enjoyed for more than half a century. In all human probability this is the last time our faltering tongues will ever tell you on an anniversary of our freedom, the story of our sufferings. May the Almighty strengthen you with virtue to defend your inheritance against foreign invasion, as well as against domestic intrigue and military usurpation.[5]

Such addresses were received with respect tinged with awe at hearing from the lips of a participant about great events that had taken place long, long ago. Naturally, the higher the rank of the ancient patriot attending a celebration, the more exciting his presence was. The highlight of the procession in Baltimore in 1820 was the presence of Charles Carroll, a signer of the original document, who carried a copy of the Declaration, which he presented to the Reader of the Day.[6]

In view of the persistent difficulties Washington encountered with recruiting enough men to field an army, the number of nonagenarian veterans who attended Fourth of July celebrations even into the 1850s is astonishing. In Providence, Rhode Island on July 5, 1830 (the Fourth fell on Sunday), no fewer than 60 Revolutionary War veterans rode in a special carriage 36 feet long, drawn by eight horses. And even the small city of Newburgh, New York boasted eight Revolutionary veterans at its celebration in 1839, when the youngest veteran would have been 74 years old—if he had been a 15-year-old boy at the battle of Yorktown—and most of them must have been nearer 90.[7] In 1847, an ancient soldier was introduced in Indianapolis to a holiday crowd who were told to look carefully, for this might be the last hero of the struggle for Independence they would ever see.[8] Yet as late as 1858 the city of Cleveland invited a 98-year-old veteran to attend the Fourth of July celebrations.[9]

No one inquired too closely into the credentials of so large a number of veterans from so small an army since everyone was delighted by their presence. Mothers held their small children up to see or shake hands with a man who had actually stood and fought with the great Washington, and the Orator of the Day could turn, extend his arm toward the venerable soldiers and exclaim, as the Orator at Syracuse, New York did in 1852, "God Almighty Bless you, for having taught us how to enjoy, and how to defend our freedom."[10] On July Fourth, 1828, the proprietors of the Baltimore and Ohio Railroad managed to combine the custom of dedicating new enterprises on Independence Day with the tradition of honoring survivors of the Revolutionary generation, when 91-year-old Charles Carroll turned the first earth at Gwynns Falls, Maryland to begin building a railroad that would cross the mountains and reach the Ohio in 1852.

Sectarian Dinners

Although American political tempers had cooled considerably since the era of heated rivalry preceding the War of 1812, partisan ferment had not entirely disappeared. From the 1820s onward, most towns managed to hold patriotic exercises on the Fourth of July that excluded no party, confining politics to toasting rival candidates and party heroes after the Fourth of July dinner. Since men who have drunk 20, 40, or more toasts, will fail to act with circumspection when they hear their political heroes insulted by partisans of a rival party, many towns that managed to hold unified exercises in the sober morning hours found it expedient to allow party loyalty to determine the guest list for the afternoon's holiday dinners. Separate, partisan Fourth of July exercises, as well as separate dinners, continued to be held in other towns through the 1840s.

Dinner might be anything from the formal gatherings in eastern towns at which important elected officials, members of the Society of Cincinnati, and other prominant gentlemen sat at table together, to informal barbecues at which an entire frontier community gathered to celebrate the day. But a dinner was essential and the dinner always ended with toasts. Even in areas, particularly in the South and on the frontier, where ladies dined with the gentlemen, the ladies would excuse themselves when the toasting began—although they might withdraw only as far as a nearby room or grove, and send in toasts to the men. At dinner on the Fourth of July 1827, in Poplar Springs, Georgia, the gentlemen managed to drink 100 toasts, no fewer than 32 of which were sent in by the ladies.[11]

Fervent patriotism was the note struck by Fourth of July toasts, which tended to be long-winded and grandiose. The first toast was usually offered in honor of:

> The Day—It opened a new era in the annals of the world—may the principles which gave birth to virtuous liberty be cherished and perpetuated, until the day when a regeneration, approximating man still nearer to the great Creator, shall arrive.[12]

This pompous toast, offered in Detroit in 1823, is representative of the genre and of a generation that liked speechifying so well that it was not unheard of for the after-dinner program to include two or three speeches to supplement the morning's oration.

During the first half-century of independence, the Fourth of July was a day on which men in the company of other men engaged in the male pleasures of admiring the military, reveling in politics, and getting drunk. Women interrupted this masculine revel only once, when the 13th toast was drunk in their honor—not their presence.

In the 1820s, Fourth of July celebrations began, very gradually, to include women. They were first admitted as observers during the morning's formal exercises and, very occasionally, as young girls acting symbolic roles in the Fourth of July procession.[13] There could be no question of admitting ladies to the gentlemen's dinner with its drunken toasts, but the evening hours were unclaimed and it was here that the ladies began to invade the male holiday.

In 1825, the ladies of Pittsfield, Massachusetts invited the gentlemen to an evening tea party in a bower near the village.[14] Tea parties were held in other towns, but they were not nearly as popular as dances. In the larger towns of Ohio, Indiana, Kentucky, Missouri, Michigan and other western states, nightfall on the Fourth of July was likely to see young people gathering at a hotel or taverr for a lively evening of dancing and flirtation.[15]

The Nation's 50th Birthday

As the Fourth of July 1826, approached, there was a general impulse to celebrate the Jubilee of Independence. And truly, Americans had much to celebrate. Thirteen colonies had become a successful nation of 24 states, which, with western territories, stretched from the Atlantic to the Oregon coast of the Pacific. Despite gloomy European views on the likely failure of a republican government, the United States could boast 50 years of independence with liberty and democratic institutions intact.

In retrospect, we see a nation in which the population was increasing, where steamboats plied the rivers, American ships sailed the seven seas, and new canals, roads and factories opened every week. A nation, that is, on the verge of unprecedented wealth, power and industrial might. This was not apparent in 1826. America was still a nation of farmers, and dwellers in small towns and seaports dedicated to serving the needs of farmers. Americans were far prouder of the political liberties they held, undiminished, as a heritage from the revolutionary generation, than of the industrial and commercial future opening up before them. As the Jubilee approached, a prosperous nation prepared to celebrate the glorious spirit of 1776.

Fifty years is a long time. Few of those who prepared to celebrate the Jubilee were old enough to recall the events of 1776. Yet 50 years was also short enough time that a handful of the prime actors in the dramatic events of that year were still alive as the national Jubilee approached. John Adams, foremost colonial spokesman for independence, lived in his comfortable home at Quincy. He was 91 years old. Thomas Jefferson, author of the Declaration of Independence, lived at his beautiful Monticello. He was 83. Charles Carroll of Carrollton, who had signed the Declaration as a representative of Maryland, was a spry 89. No general officers of the American Army were still living, but Lafayette, who had enjoyed a triumphal tour of the United States in 1824–25, still lived in France. The Jubilee was celebrated in honor of these aging heroes and their Revolutionary comrades, living and dead.

Towns throughout the nation held meetings to plan Fourth of July celebrations that would follow the familiar outline but be a little more grand than in an ordinary year.

Special efforts were made to secure the participation of Revolutionary veterans. Quincy, Massachusetts, naturally hoped that John Adams would attend the public exercises, but declining health prevented him from accepting the invitation. The committee delegated to arrange the celebration called on the aging patriot to request that he compose a toast to be given at the dinner in his name. "I give you," he replied, "INDEPENDENCE FOREVER." Asked if he wished to add something further, Adams firmly replied "Not a word."

Jefferson and Adams, the two Revolutionary collaborators turned partisan rivals, had put their political differences behind them and become friends in old age, as they were in youth. The parties they had headed remained at loggerheads, but the letters that flowed regularly between Quincy and Monticello were warm and intimate, revealing one of the most beautiful friendships in American history.

At Washington, the 13 members of the Committee of Arrangements determined to celebrate the Jubilee by inviting all living signers of the Declaration of Independence and all surviving former presidents to Fourth of July exercises in the city. The august group included Adams, Jefferson, Carroll, James Madison and James Monroe. None of the aging patriots was able to attend, but the letters of regret sent by each were widely reprinted in the newspapers. President John Quincy Adams, reading the replies, was pleased to note that his ancient father had managed to sign the letter himself and that Charles Carroll's letter was in his own handwriting. But the vigor of Jefferson's response amazed President Adams and thrilled the nation.

> Respected Sir:
> The kind invitation I received from you, on the part of the citizens of the city of Washington, to be present with them at their celebration of the Fiftieth Anniversary of American Independence, as one of the surviving signers of an instrument, pregnant with our own and with the fate of the world, is most flattering to myself, . . . It adds sensibly to the sufferings of sickness to be deprived by it of a personal participation in the rejoicings of that day, . . . I should, indeed, with peculiar delight, have met and exchanged there congratulations, personally, with the small band, the remnant of that host of worthies who joined with us on that day, in the bold and doubtful election we were to make, for our country, between

A humorous view of the cannon explosions that all too frequently marred the holiday. (Circa 1830 print by William Pendleton, Boston. Collection of the American Antiquarian Society, Worcester.)

submission and the sword; and to have enjoyed with them the consolatory fact that our fellow citizens, after half a century of experience and prosperity, continue to approve the choice we made. May it be to the world, what I believe it will be, (to some parts sooner, to others later, but finally to all,) the signal of arousing men to burst the chains under which monkish ignorance and superstition had persuaded them to bind themselves, and to assume the blessings and security of self-government. . . . let the annual return of this day forever refresh our recollections of these rights, and an undiminished devotion to them.[16]

It is poignant to think of these aging patriots, still alive to see the 50th anniversary of the nation they formed but prevented by the infirmity of age from the pleasure of greeting the comrades of youth one last time. Throughout the nation, orators paid tribute, partisan differences were put aside and glasses were raised to toast the heroes of 1776.

Citizens of Newark, New Jersey, like Americans everywhere, awoke at dawn to the boom of cannon and the clamor of church bells. By mid-morning the procession had formed. In the van, 60 Revolutionary War veterans, one in complete uniform, the others attired in such fragments of uniforms and assorted guns, cartridge boxes and powder horns as they possessed and had managed to preserve. Following the veterans were the local militia and an orderly procession of trade groups: tailors, blacksmiths, quarrymen, stonecutters and masons, carpenters, curriers, shoemakers, coach makers, cabinetmakers, chair makers, saddlers and painters. These were followed by the Committee of Arrangements, bearers of the Cap of Liberty and Standard, the Orator and Reader of the Declaration, Clergymen, city officials and citizens, all of whom attended the formal exercises of the day in a church.

After the exercises, the Revolutionary veterans led a procession that included ox teams dragging a 50-foot obelisk to a site where it was erected as a monument to "Independence and Government." Not content with a single monument, the citizens of Newark also dedicated that day a Temple of Independence on the town common. This edifice had 13 columns supporting a domed roof topped by a fleur-de-lis. Around the top were inscribed "Independence," "Fourth of July," "1776," and "Liberty and Equality," while names of Revolutionary War generals were written around the outer ring. After a day of dedications, Newark enjoyed a grand illumination in the evening, as 13 barrels of tar were set ablaze to light the common, and candles and torches illuminated the public buildings, flagstaff, the new temple and the quarry.[17]

The Fourth of July was to be the occasion for the dedication of patriotic monuments by generations of Americans. On July 4, 1848, the cornerstone was laid for the Washington Monument in the District of Columbia, in ceremonies presided over by President James Polk and attended by Dolly Madison.

While the nation celebrated and toasted his deeds, Jefferson lay dying at Monticello. Overtaken by his final illness on July second, this great man roused himself late on the evening of the third to ask a young relative, "Is it the Fourth?"

Those were his final words. Thomas Jefferson departed this life at one in the afternoon on the 50th anniversary of Independence. Informed on July sixth of the passing of Jefferson, President John Quincy Adams commented on the "strange and very striking coincidence," a sentiment shared by every American who had heard the news. It was to become more striking still.

On the morning of the Fourth of July 1826, John Adams took his usual chair in his upstairs study at home in Quincy. He passed the day very quietly, able to hear through the windows the noise of the Quincy celebration and the cheers when the toast he had sent was proposed. During the afternoon he said to his granddaughter, though speech for him by then was slow and difficult, "Thomas Jefferson survives." Toward six in the evening, this noble patriot died. Having received word of his father's rapidly sinking health, his son raced home; he was told the news at an inn near Baltimore. America was stunned, immediately interpreting the deaths, as John Quincy Adams did, as a "visible and palpable" manifestation of "Divine favor" toward John Adams, Thomas Jefferson and the nation they had created.

In cities and villages that summer and fall, Americans gathered to memorialize the two great patriots. Orators rose to the occasion by avoiding partisan references in their eulogies, speaking instead of the values the two men shared, the beauty of their friendship and the lessons that the nation could draw from their lives.

Notes

1. *Onondaga Register*, July 23, 1817.
2. *Herald* (Cleveland), July 6, 1827.
3. Henry A. Hawken, *Trumpets of Glory; Fourth of July Orations, 1786–1861*, Chapter 5, Salmon Brook Historical Society, Granby, Conn., 1986.
4. *Cleveland Herald*, July 9, 1824; "The Republican Sentiment of New-Hampshire, July 4, 1828, exhibited in her anniversary celebrations," pamphlet in the collection of the American Antiquarian Society, Worcester, Mass.
5. *Niles Weekly Register*, August 16, 1828.
6. *Niles Weekly Register*, July 8, 1820, p. 329.
7. *Providence Journal*, July 5, 1830; *Niles Weekly Register*, July 20, 1839, p. 336.
8. *Diary of Calvin Fletcher*, edited by Gayle Thornbrough, Indiana Historical Society, Indianapolis, 1972, July 4, 1847.
9. *Cleveland Leader*, June 30, 1858.
10. Quoted in Robert Pettus Hay, *Freedom's Jubilee*, p. 79.

11. Robert Pettus Hay, *Freedom's Jubilee*, p. 112.

12. *Detroit Gazette*, July 11, 1823, reprinted in the *Historical Collections* of the Michigan Pioneer and Historical Society Report of the Annual Meeting of 1889, p. 527; a full discussion of Fourth of July toasts is given in Hay, *Freedom's Jubilee*.

13. Fletcher M. Green, "Listen to the Eagle Scream," *North Carolina Historical Review*, July 1854, p. 307; *Herald* (Cleveland), July 16, 1824; *Brookville Enquirer* (Indiana) July 2, 1819; *Diary of Calvin Fletcher* edited by Gayle Thornbrough, entry and footnote for July 4, 1822, Indiana Historical Society, Indianapolis, 1972.

14. *Pittsfield Sun* (Massachusetts), July 7, 1825; *Farmer's Repository* (Charleston, West Virginia), July 6, 1815.

15. *Missouri Intelligencer* (Franklin), July 1, 1823, reprinted in *Missouri Historical Review* July 1, 1924, p. 614; *Detroit Gazette*, July 11, 1823, reprinted in *Historical Collections of the Michigan Pioneer and Historical Society* Report of the Annual Meeting of 1889, p. 572; *Herald* (Cleveland), July 14, 1826; *Diary of Calvin Fletcher*, Gayle Thornbrough, editor, entry for July 4, 1822, Indiana Historical Society, Indianapolis, 1972; Hay, "Jubilee for Freemen," p. 174.

16. L. H. Butterfield, "The Jubilee of Independence," *The Virginia Magazine of History and Biography*, April, 1953; see also Robert P. Hay, "The Glorious Departure of the American Patriarchs," *Journal of Southern History*, November, 1969.

17. "The First Jubilee of American Independence and Tribute of Gratitude to the Illustrious Adams and Jefferson, Newark, New Jersey," Newark, 1826, pamphlet in the collection of the American Antiquarian Society, Worcester.

Cold Water and Liberty 6

In the 1830s and '40s, the Fourth of July became the occasion of "religious exercises, temperance orations and colonization addresses."[1] The holiday still featured processions, exercises and dinners, but the slogans on the banners carried in procession, the topic of the orations and the nature of the toasts all changed.

In the agrarian society of federal America, drinking had been as normal as eating. Hard cider was the ordinary beverage at the family table for breakfast no less than dinner, and it was cider and ale that quenched the thirst of laborers in field and workshop. The tavern was the center of social life in town. In fact, it was often the only public gathering place aside from the church.

The church did not frown on drinking until the 1830s. Federal and colonial ministers drank spirits as freely as their flocks; they were expected to serve liquor to their visiting parishioners, and at such church celebrations as ordinations, visiting clergymen refreshed themselves with cider, ale and rum. If men who daily drank sizable quantities of alcohol chose, on an occasional holiday, to raise their cups in patriotic toasts until they were rolling drunk, this behavior was not seriously disruptive to the social order. Some patriots might have to be helped home to sleep it off, but there were friends around to aid them. Some jobs might go undone the morning after, but they could be done later in the week. Drinking, and the fact that drinking will occasionally lead to drinking to excess, were simple facts of life. With the growth of cities and the beginning of large-scale industry, attitudes began to change.

Independence from Alcohol

Factories that required a full complement of workers to operate machines every morning at sunrise could not accommodate workmen who needed the morning after to sleep off a drinking bout. And while residents of small towns could indulge the occasional drunkenness of a familiar neighbor, or even of a large group of familiar neighbors, residents of cities feared the drunken potential of the thousands of strangers among whom they lived.

It was out of the needs of industry and the fears of residents of the rapidly growing cities that the temperance movement was born. The first advocates of temperance, in the mid-1820s, were men of substance who literally advocated "temperance," that is, moderation in the use of intoxicating spirits. Within a decade, these moderate gentlemen were superceded by a more broadly based coalition enthusiastically advocating total abstinence, which became known as teetotalism. Abstinence inspired enthusiasm in a way that moderation never had, and by the early 1840s, a working-class leadership had emerged at the head of a total abstinence movement rapidly spreading its gospel across the nation.

Getting men to pledge total abstinence was never easy, even in a generation that had made abstinence fashionable, but encouraging men to live up to their pledges was more difficult still. The tavern was a ma, ʾr center of social life; indeed, wherever men gathered, liquor was served. Theateɩ ʒ and bowling alleys served drinks. Alcohol was served at militia drills, formal public dinners, and informal gatherings to watch a boxing match or cock fight.

No place of amusement was free of alcohol so the teetotalers sponsored amusements of their own and promoted cold water as the drink of choice. There were teetotal lectures, of course, but there were also teetotal hotels, balls at which no intoxicating drink was served and concerts where teetotal singers presented such popular tunes as "I've Thrown the Bowl Aside," and "Sparkling with Light is the Water Bright."[2] Among these alternative amusements was the Fourth of July picnic, an annual highlight of every teetotal society.

Patriotic toasting, a central Fourth of July tradition, was dealt with forthrightly by the teetotalers: they toasted in lemonade[3] or they toasted in cold water:

> Let us drink to the President, long life and good health,
> To the people, rich streams of the sources of wealth.
> May the Army and Navy uphold the good cause,
> Our good Constitution, our Freedom and Laws,
> So sparkle each eye and let every heart bound,
> To fill high your glasses, and send the toast round.
> But hark ye—don't fill them with brandy, nor beer;
> But water, pure water, the very best cheer—
> By such a potation, 'twill ever be found,
> Constitution and laws are kept healthy and sound.[4]

Temperance celebrations poured new content into traditional forms. There were processions that featured temperance groups carrying colorful banners to sites selected for Fourth of July exercises. After the traditional reading of the Declaration of Independence, there were songs and odes, the songs on temperance themes and the odes in honor of temperance as well as Independence. And there were orations. A common theme was the need for a second Declaration of Independence—the first proclaimed liberty from King George, the second freedom from King Alcohol.[5] The exercises were followed by picnics and toasts in cold water.

In many towns, members of the Total Abstinence or Temperance Societies were joined by children pledged to life-long teetotalism and organized into a Cold Water Army. Carrying abstinence banners and flags they had crafted themselves, the children marched to picnic groves where they were regaled with stories of the contrast between the tottering, diseased, intellectually enfeebled debauchee and the vigor of a man who had never known strong drink—before being led to the amply spread picnic tables.[6]

Temperance advocates and backers of the Sunday school movement had latched onto ways of making a popular holiday promote the causes they advocated. It was a tactic that soon became as traditional on the Fourth of July as reading the Declaration and shooting off fireworks.

The Sunday School Celebrations

The Sunday school movement was part of a general resurgence of American Protestantism in the early 19th century. Although some American Sunday schools were designed, like British ones, to provide a basic education to children who worked on weekdays, most American Sunday schools were intended to improve the religious knowledge and piety of children who learned to read and write in public schools. The Sunday school movement spread rapidly across the country, achieving tremendous popularity.

The Fourth of July Sunday school outing, which, in the 1830s, quickly became an American institution, was a treat planned to reward the boys and girls for a year's dutiful study. Part of the intention of the planners, who were usually advocates of temperance, was to remove children from the spectacle of heavy drinking at the public celebrations in town. Equally important was the general Victorian impulse to view childhood as a special stage of life, and children as creatures who ought to have entertainments of their own, separate from those of the adult world. The result was that throughout the nation, Sunday school children were marched off to Fourth of July celebrations apart from the adult ceremonies.

These celebrations closely echoed traditional adult exercises. In the morning, the children would form up and march two-by-two to a church or large hall where children from several churches could gather, or they might march directly to the grove where the picnic would be held in the countryside. Either way, the day's activities began with formal exercises, including an oration, songs and a reading of the Declaration. Then there were refreshments before the children reformed their lines and marched back to town. Organized sports for children's outings were a later innovation.[7]

The Bombs Bursting in Air

Fireworks, gunpowder and noise in all forms had become prominent features of the Fourth. By nightfall on the third of July, a constant din of firecrackers, bombs, rockets, pistols, drums and trumpets had begun that would not subside until long after midnight on the Fourth. Boys were not permitted to throw lighted firecrackers through open windows or at the feet of passersby, although they regularly did, but the purchase and use of firecrackers and fireworks was perfectly legal. A number of cities went so far as to suspend ordinances against discharging firearms within the city limits in honor of the Fourth of July.[8] Making noise was a Fourth of July tradition pursued vigorously in cities like New York, where the municipal authorities provided a good deal of racket for the populace in the form of cannon salutes, ringing bells, fireworks and military band concerts, and in small towns like Troy, Wisconsin, where an early settler recalled that on the Fourth of July, 1837, "There were only three of us in town and one gun, but we fired the gun."[9]

In large towns the militia fired cannon, military companies fired salutes, revenue cutters and naval ships fired cannonades, and citizens pointed their guns skyward and fired at will. The din was tremendous. When the USS *Constitution*, "Old Ironsides," pride of the United States Navy, was in New York for the Fourth of July 1835, it fired a salute from its mighty cannon that could scarcely

A Fourth of July picnic at Weston Park in Weymouth, Massachusetts in the 1840s, painted by Susan Torrey Merritt. (Courtesy of the Art Institute of Chicago)

be heard above the clamor of the city.[10] A pall of gunpowder hung over cities and villages throughout the day as men and boys expressed their noisy pleasure in independence.[11]

Guns were everywhere in use on the Fourth, but in addition to employing guns owned by the household for other purposes, small boys were often presented with little two-pound cannons that could be filled with gunpowder and ignited to make a splendid bang. Lacking gun or cannon, a boy could improvise: Rutherford B. Hayes was a student at Kenyon College in Ohio when he celebrated the Fourth of July by pouring a charge of powder into a log. Hayes succeeded in making a loud noise and, incidentally, split the log.[12]

Firecrackers and manufactured fireworks rarely reached small towns and rural areas in the 1830s, so country folk continued to shoot their Fourth of July gunpowder straight from the gun.[13] If no cannon was available for official salutes, citizens of a small town could make do by "firing an anvil." Two anvils were needed. The first was placed on the ground and its cavity filled with black powder with a fuse laid across it. The second anvil was then placed upside down on top of the first. When the fuse was lit, the top anvil would rise high into the air with a report that sounded very much like a cannon. Of course, if there was a flaw in the iron the anvil might explode and pass through the crowd like grapeshot.[14] Fires, death and mutilation caused by misfiring or exploding guns and cannon were a predictable part of the annual celebration.

The Question of Black Freedom

The noise, and even the evening fireworks display that had become common in the larger towns, were still only background for the formal exercises that continued to keynote the day's festivities, which featured speeches, patriotic songs and odes to liberty. Speakers of the early 1830s were struck by the remarkable coincidence of the death of President James Monroe at his daughter's home in New York on July 4, 1831. Of the four deceased former presidents, all but Washington had died on the Fourth of July.

On July 4, 1824, the Reverend Leonard Bacon of Center Church, New Haven was in Boston to deliver a sermon on the topic of African colonization. It was the first in what was to be a long series of Fourth of July colonization sermons inspired by the efforts of Ralph Randolph Gurley, a young man with a genius for promoting the cause he believed in;[15] that cause was the foundation of an African colony as a home for free blacks from the United States—the land that became Liberia.

Liberia today is an independent nation, but it began as the vision of a small group of American philanthropists. Some of the sponsors of the American

Flags wave, the militia parades, boys fire pistols, and street vendors hawk fireworks in a free-wheeling celebration of the Fourth of July, 1834. (Looking South on Broadway from corner of Cortland Street, 1934, drawn by Dan Beard. Harper's Weekly, July 7, 1894)

Colonization Society were slaveholders who viewed the presence of a small but growing number of free blacks on American soil as a threat to their peculiar institution. The success of black freemen might undermine the ideology of racial inferiority that was an important part of the rationale for black chattel slavery. Even more threatening was the possibility that the mere presence of black freemen might stir discontent among the slaves. Better to remove the free blacks to Africa before they could cause trouble.

Other supporters of colonization were antislavery men and women who believed that if there were a land where freed slaves could go, more slave owners might be encouraged to free their slaves. In fact, a handful of slave owners did free or will their slaves to the Colonization Society, with the understanding that the freed slaves would become colonists in Africa.

Whether motivated by a desire to preserve slavery or to end it, supporters of African colonization saw their efforts as an act of benevolence toward the free blacks who would be helped to establish themselves in Africa. Both groups of sponsors disliked the idea of having free blacks living side by side with white people in American cities and saw removal as the solution, but it took large amounts of money to transport colonists to Africa and outfit a colony. Gurley came up with the clever idea of asking ministers to preach Fourth of July sermons on African colonization and take up collections to aid the colonists.

Through the 1820s and 1830s, Colonization Society meetings and colonization sermons and orations were a common fixture of Fourth of July festivities. The Springfield, Massachusetts Colonization Society met at Dr. Osgood's meeting house on July 4, 1829; they heard an address on colonization, prayed, sang several hymns and collected $81 to assist the colonists. Henry Ward Beecher's church in Lawrenceburgh, Indiana managed to collect only $19 and change, but the overall result was that several thousand dollars in badly needed contributions could be counted to fill the society's coffers after the annual Fourth of July appeals.[16]

While it was indeed possible to plant a successful colony of free American blacks on African soil, the colonization movement declined as abolition came to the fore. Most free American blacks did not wish to go to Africa—and, whatever the desires of the small number of free blacks in America, colonization could not end slavery.

Even in colonial times, there were a few lonely voices raised in opposition to black slavery, and there was significant antislavery sentiment during the Revolutionary era, which led several northern states to abolish slavery. But a serious abolition movement did not begin to gather momentum in this country until the 1830s, after British abolitionists had shown the way. The movement gained momentum, too, with the invention of a gin that could mechanically separate seeds from cotton fiber making slave labor on cotton plantations hugely profitable, and destroying any hope that slavery in the South might simply wither away as it had in the northern states.

Nothing could be more appropriate than for the Fourth of July to be dedicated to the abolitionist cause. This was the holiday on which generations of Americans gathered at crossroads churches and county courthouses to hear readings of Mr. Jefferson's immortal Declaration, "That all men are created equal, that they are endowed by their Creator with certain inalienable rights, that among these rights are life, liberty, and the pursuit of happiness. ...

Abolition was first called "immediate emancipation," and the earliest ideological battles fought by advocates of immediate emancipation were not against slave holders, but against those who proposed to end slavery through African colonization. The people of the small town of Elyria, Ohio gathered on the Fourth of July 1833, to hear a debate between Immediate Abolitionists and advocates of the American Colonization Society. About 400 citizens, including many who had walked or ridden several miles from farms in the surrounding countryside, gathered at the Elyria Court House to hear a reading of the Declaration of Independence and listen to a band play patriotic songs before the debate began. The disputants were ministers, lawyers, physicians and other prominent citizens. Some read carefully prepared speeches, and some spoke passionately, without notes, in a debate that lasted all day, with only an hour break for lunch.[17] We don't know if there was a winner in the Elyria debate, but the immediate emancipationists soon took the clear lead in American antislavery activity.

In 1832, William Lloyd Garrison published his pamphlet Thoughts on Colonization, which contained the famous abolitionist's arguments opposing colonization. In 1833, Americans inspired by the passage of the British Abolition Act founded the New York Anti-Slavery Society and, later in the year, the first national antislavery society.

Opponents of slavery throughout the nation soon ceased to debate the merits of colonization and moved to form antislavery organizations. In 1837, a group of citizens of Cleveland, "Believing that the Declaration of July 4, 1776, which led to the redemption of three millions of people from British thraldom, cannot be more appropriately commemorated than by exertions to rescue three millions of the present generation from bondage ten times more intolerable," invited the "friends of Universal Liberty" to join them at the Stone Church on the morning of the Fourth of July to form a Cuyahoga County Anti-Slavery Society.[18]

Other antislavery societies also held their meetings on July Fourth, and it is not surprising that the conscientiously progressive community of Oberlin College in Ohio devoted itself to abolitionist activity on the Fourth of July.[19] Some antislavery societies held Fourth of July picnics.[20] Although abolition picnics never attained the popularity of temperance picnics, even in such hotbeds of abolitionist sentiment as Massachusetts, they did set a standard for inflammatory rhetoric in aid of a cause.

Speaking at abolitionist Fourth of July exercises in Framingham, Massachusetts in 1854, abolitionist William Lloyd Garrison condemned the Fugitive Slave Law, emphasizing his point by burning a copy of the law. He then condemned the Constitution of the United States as a "covenant with death and agreement with hell," and electrified the audience by holding a copy of the Constitution aloft and setting it ablaze as he proclaimed, "So perish all compromises with tyranny," while the audience shouted "Amen."[21]

Abolition was not popular. Many who agreed that enslaving blacks was wrong also felt that abolitionists were troublemakers. And blacks were even less popular than abolitionists. American society in the 1830s was thoroughly segregated, with blacks, even in free states, given inferior legal status and very inferior social status. Even Americans who opposed slavery were appalled by any notion of racial equality or integration, and new or growing black settlements often met opposition.

Among the leading abolitionists, however, were individuals unique in their generation because they sincerely favored racial integration. As part of their commitment to racial equality, abolitionists admitted black and white members to their societies on a equal footing and invited black speakers to sit beside white on the platform at abolitionist gatherings. Integration of this sort offended the sensibilities of most Americans and sometimes unleashed the fury of an anti-black mob.

The New York Anti-Slavery Society met, as scheduled, on the morning of July 4, 1834, to hold integrated exercises in the Chatham Street Chapel. When hecklers disrupted the celebration, it was rescheduled for July seventh. On that night, the integrated exercises were again broken up by a white mob in a melee that set off a week of rioting—the worst riots that New York City saw up to the time of the Civil War.[22]

The principles of the abolitionists clashed violently with public opinion. Americans were viscerally opposed to social mixing of the races, especially since social mingling might lead to interracial marriage, the very suggestion of which was horrifying to public sentiment. But true to their principles, abolitionists moved to invite black speakers to address mixed audiences on the Fourth of July and so make a statement for justice. To the prejudiced majority, an integrated program was an affront and a provocation.

The authorities were likely to view as provocateurs the abolitionists who sponsored integrated public exercises, not the rioters who broke them up. The New York *Courier and Enquirer* was clear in its condemnation of the abolitionists whose integrated celebration incensed the New York mob of July 1834. "Now we tell them, that when they openly and publicly promulgate doctrines which outrage public feeling, they have no right to demand protection

An abolitionist view of the Fourth of July under slavery. The caption reads: "Behold! the degraded son of Africa, reading the Declaration of Independence, handcuffed as he is; and stared at with astonishment by the Husband and Wife, in front of him, who are also chained; and whose appearance seems to say, 'are these things so.' The Musicians, no doubt, could perform better, at least with more ease to themselves, if they had the use of both hands. On the back ground is to be seen, the notorious Judge Linch, with whip in hand, and his foot on the Constitution,—bolstered up with bales of Cotton and hogsheads of Tobacco—surrounded by his Mob Court, condemning the friends of humanity, and executing them upon the spot, merely for supporting that clause of the Declaration, vi : 'All men are created free and equal,' and acting in conformity with 192 passages of Holy writ, which are either directly or indirectly, against the system of SLAVERY." (By William Rhinehart, collection of the American Antiquarian Society, Worcester, Mass.)

from the people they thus insult."[23] Nor did the mayor of New York rush to provide police protection for the president of the New York Anti-slavery Society, whose home was destroyed in the riot, or for the homes and churches of ministers who had spoken in favor of abolition. The greatest destruction was in the black neighborhoods, where police were similarly absent.

Although abolitionist Fourth of July exercises and picnics often proceeded without event, they were sometimes, as they had been in New York, the occasion of anti-black riots. When a Fourth of July crowd of young men, collected from nearby villages and the surrounding countryside, drinking to patriotic toasts, and firing off guns and pistols in patriotic fervor, heard that a group of "nigger lovers" were sullying the national festival by holding integrated exercises, a mob was easily roused.

In 1843, a white mob tore down a school in Caanan, New Hampshire where black students had been invited to speak from the platform with white students during Fourth of July exercises.[24] And on July 4, 1845, a drunken reveler began taunting a black man who was merely walking down a street in Indianapolis. A crowd gathered and joined in taunting the black man who finally hit back, whereupon the crowd turned murderous and bludgeoned the black man to death.[25] As late as 1903, an ugly, racist mob tore through the black neighborhood of Evansville, Illinois on the Fourth of July. And in 1908, when celebrating crowds learned that Jack Johnson, the first black heavyweight champion, had bested a white opponent in a celebrated July 4 prize fight, anti-black riots broke out in cities throughout the nation.[26]

The threat of rioting by drunken Fourth of July mobs probably induced some blacks in racially tense cities to stay quietly at home on the Fourth of July, but many blacks would have stayed at home in any case. In the ringing words of black abolitionist and orator Frederick Douglass, "This Fourth of July is *yours*, not *mine*. *You* may rejoice, *I* must mourn. To drag a man in fetters into the grand, illuminated temple of liberty, and call upon him to join you in joyous anthems, were inhuman mockery and sacrilegious irony."

Douglass, who delivered this famous speech at a Fourth of July celebration in Rochester, New York, asked his audience, "Do you mean, citizens, to mock me, by asking me to speak today?" and drew for them the Biblical parallel with the Jews carried into captivity by the rivers of Babylon who "hanged our harps upon the willow . . . for there they that carried us away captive, required of us a song; and they who wasted us, required of us mirth . . ."[27]

Douglass' parallel was precise, for American slaveholders were in fact in the habit of allowing their slaves to celebrate the Fourth of July as a holiday. On many plantations Independence Day and Christmas were the major holidays of the year. On some plantations, the slaves were allowed to act as hosts at a picnic for slaves from neighboring plantations, at which slaves would play patriotic music and sometimes even deliver patriotic Fourth of July orations. The irony of giving Independence Day as a holiday to slaves apparently escaped the plantation owners.[28]

Free blacks perceived the irony. For the most part, they chose not to celebrate the Fourth of July, and some abolitionists joined them in refusing to celebrate the Independence Day of a nation that enslaved so many of its own people.[29] Independence Day, 1827 was an exception to this rule, for on that day a law ending slavery in the state of New York went into effect. Black communities throughout the state held Fourth of July exercises that year; they were of the traditional type with orations and readings of the Declaration of Independence. In an innovation on the custom of firing a salute in honor of every state, the black community in one New York town fired a salute in honor of each state in which slavery was illegal.[30]

Black reluctance to celebrate July Fourth was strong. For several years after 1827, some black communities in New York celebrated a holiday on July 5th, marking their freedom while still expressing their reservations about the national Independence Day. Other black communities celebrated January 1st, the day when the foreign slave trade was abolished in 1808, but the most popular alternative in the 1830's and afterwards was to celebrate the anniversary of August 1st, 1834, the day when slavery was abolished in the British Empire.[31]

Popular as the Sunday school and temperance celebrations were, and fervent as the abolitionists were in their cause, these remained auxiliary events, not the central celebration of Independence Day. Throughout the 1830s, small towns and large cities held formal, public ceremonies at which public officials and distinguished citizens marched in procession to formal exercises in honor of the day. Temperance, abolition and Sunday school exercises held in addition to these official exercises did not supplant the official event, but they were a sign that the times were changing.

Notes

1. Cleveland *Herald* editorial of July 13, 1833.
2. Ian Tyrrell, *Sobering Up: From Temperance to Prohibition in Antebellum American, 1800–1860*, Greenwood Press, Westport, Conn. 1979, pp. 177–179.
3. *Diary and Letters of Rutherford Birchard Hayes*, letter of July 9, 1839.
4. "A Cold Water Toast," dated 1837, in *The Fourth of July Book* by "A Sunday School Man."
5. Ian Tyrell, *Sobering Up*, p. 179.

6. Mary A. Livermore, *The Story of My Life*, A. D. Worthington, and Co. Hartford, 1898, pp. 377–378; Cleveland *Herald*, July 5, 1843; and *Diary of Calvin Fletcher*, entry for July 4, 1843.

7. *Diary of Calvin Fletcher*, Gayle Thornbrough, editor, Indiana Historical Society, Indianapolis, 1972, entries for July 4 in the 1830s and 1840s; *Herald and Gazette* (Cleveland), July 5, 1838; *The Fourth of July Book; Containing Plans for a Juvenile Observance of the National Festival with Hymns, Songs and Recitations Adapted to such Occasions* by "A Sunday School Man," Office of the Sabbath School Monitor, Piercy and Reed, Printers, New York, 1841, penny tract in the collection of the Boston Public Library; and Elizabeth Hayward, *John M'Coy; His Life and His Diaries*, American Historical Company, Inc., New York, 1948, entries for July 4, 1842 and 1851.

8. See, for example, annual notices in the *Cleveland Herald*.

9. Lillian Kruger, "Social Life in Wisconsin, Pre-Territorial through the Mid-Sixties," *The Wisconsin Magazine of History*, June, 1939.

10. *The Diary of Philip Hone*, Allan Nevins, editor, Dodd, Mead, and Co., New York, 1927, entry for July 4, 1835.

11. Robert Pettus Hay, *Britons in New York on Brother Jonathan's Birthday*, New-York Historical Society Quarterly, July, 1969.

12. *Diary and Letters of Rutherford Birchard Hayes*, Charles Richard Williams, editor, Ohio State Archeological and Historical Society, 1922, entry for July 4, 1841; accounts of Hayes' boyhood use of toy Fourth of July cannon in entries for July 6, and July 11, 1841.

13. Lucy Larcom, *A New England Girlhood*, Houghton, Mifflin Co., Boston, 1889, p. 99; and Fletcher M. Green, "Listen to the Eagle Scream," *North Carolina Historical Review*, July, 1954, p. 309.

14. Elizabeth Silverthrone, *Plantation Life in Texas*, Texas A & M University Press, College Station, 1986, p. 114; and J. S. Holliday, "An Old Time Fourth of July," *The American West*, July 1968, p. 37.

15. P. J. Staudenraus, *The African Colonization Movement, 1816–1865*, Columbia University Press, New York, 1961, p. 119.

16. *Hampden Journal* (Springfield, Mass.), July 7, 1829; Jane Schaffer Elsmere, *Henry Ward Beecher, The Indiana Years, 1837–1847*, Indiana Historical Society, Indianapolis, 1973, p. 68; *Diaries of Phoebe George Bradford, 1832–1839*, W. Emerson Wilson, editor, Historical Society of Delaware, Wilmington, 1976, p. 46; and Staudenraus, *African Colonization*, p. 122.

17. D. Griffiths, Jr., *Two Years in the New Settlements of Ohio*, March of America Facsimile Series, Number 73, Ann Arbor, University Microfilms, Inc., 1966, pp. 93–98; Cleveland *Herald*, June 22, 1833.

18. *Herald and Gazette* (Cleveland), June 30, 1837.

19. Robert Samuel Fletcher, *A History of Oberlin College from its Foundation through the Civil War*, Oberlin College, Oberlin, 1943, p. 249.

20. Adin Ballou, *The Voice of Duty; An Address Delivered to the Anti-Slavery Picnic at Westminster, Massachusetts, July 4, 1843*, pamphlet in the collection of the American Antiquarian Society, Worcester, Mass.; and Leonard I. Sweet, "The Fourth of July and Black Americans in the Nineteenth Century," *Journal of Negro History*, July, 1976.

21. Roman J. Zorh, "The New England Anti-Slavery Society: Pioneer Abolition Organization," *Journal of Negro History*, July 1957, pp. 162–163; Archibald Grimké, *William Lloyd Garrison, The Abolitionist*, Funk and Wagnalls, London, 1891, p. 354; and Sweet, "The Fourth of July and Black Americans in the Nineteenth Century," p. 261.

22. Linda K. Kerber, "Abolitionists and Amalgamators: The New York City Race Riots of 1834," *New York History*, January, 1967; *Memoirs of Reverend Charles G. Finney*, A. S. Barnes, and Co., New York, 1876, pp. 324–329.

23. Quoted in Kerber, "Abolitionists and Amalgamators."

24. Leonard Sweet, "The Fourth of July and Black Americans in the Nineteenth Century," p. 263.

25. Jane Shaffer Elsmere, *Henry Ward Beecher: The Indiana Years, 1837–1847*, pp. 231–232; and *Diary of Calvin Fletcher*, entry for July 4, 1845.

26. Leonard Sweet, "The Fourth of July and Black Americans," pp. 263 and 274.

27. Frederick Douglass, "What to the Slave is the Fourth of July?" *The Black Scholar*, July/August 1976.

28. July Floyd Smith, *Slavery and Plantation Growth in Antebellum Florida, 1821–1860*, University of Florida Press, Gainesville, 1973, pp. 73–74; Orville W. Taylor, *Negro Slavery in Arkansas*, Duke University Press, Durham, 1958, pp. 144, 207; Abigail Curlee Holbrook, "A Glimpse of Life on Antebellum Slave Plantations in Texas," *Southwestern Historical Quarterly*, April, 1973, p. 378; Joe Gray Taylor, *Negro Slavery in Louisiana*, Louisiana Historical Association, Baton Rouge, 1963, pp. 127–128; Chase C. Mooney, *Slavery in Tennessee*, Indiana University Press, Bloomington, 1957, p. 89.

29. *Letters of James Gillespie Birney, 1831–1837*, Dwight L. Dumond, Editor, D. Appleton-Century Co., New York, 1938, letters of June 24th, 25th, 1842, pp. 699–701.

30. Benjamin Quarles, "Antebellum Free Blacks and the 'Spirit of '76'" *Journal of Negro History*, July 1976, p. 234.

31. Leonard Sweet, "The Fourth of July and Black Americans in the Nineteenth Century," p. 259; and Benjamin Quarles, "Antebellum Free Blacks and the 'Spirit of '76,'" p. 235.

Parodies and Parades 7

Daniel Webster gave his first Fourth of July oration in 1800, as an 18-year-old Dartmouth student, and his last on July 4th, 1851, when as secretary of state, he spoke at the cornerstone-laying ceremonies for the expansion of the Capitol building. Webster was America's greatest orator, a man who, we are told, once debated the Devil himself—and won. But the 19th century was an age of oratory. Powerful speakers were esteemed in the way sports heros are today: crowds thronged to hear them; people listened admiringly and discussed their merits; newspapers and books reprinted their words; little boys grew up hoping to be like them. When young Dan Webster made speeches to the cows in his father's New Hampshire pasture and Abe Lincoln interrupted his wood chopping to speak to an audience of trees, it was in pursuit of a goal shared by thousands of young Americans.

The quintessential small-town Fourth of July at mid-century. The militia drills in the background as an orator holds forth to a none-too-attentive crowd. (Harper's Weekly, July 6, 1867)

A Change in Taste

It was natural that orations should be given on the nation's great patriotic holiday and for decades a Fourth of July celebration without a speech was unthinkable.[1] Speakers sometimes addressed topical political subjects, but the usual Fourth of July oration spoke to the great themes of American nationhood: the sacrifices and contributions of the Founding Fathers, the Declaration of Independence and the meaning of liberty, the Constitution and the glories of freedom under law. The best of these orations would seem long-winded to a modern audience and the worst are unpalatably florid, but in its early 19th-century heyday, public speaking was a major and sincerely admired art form. When parodies of the Fourth of July oration began to appear in the 1850s, it was a sign that both public taste and the nature of the holiday were changing. Ever irreverent, *Vanity Fair* printed a parody in 1861, which, as good parodies do, gives us some idea of what the real orations were like:

> Feller Sitterzens, the Union's in danger. The black devil disunion is trooly here, starein us all squarely in the face. We must drive him back. Shall we make a 2nd Mexico of ourselves? Shall we sell our birthright for a mess of potash? Shall one brother put the knife to the throat of anuther brother? Shall we mix our whiskey with each other' blud? Shall the star spangled Banner be cut up into dishcloths? Standin here in this here Skoolhouse, upon my nativ shore so to speak, I anser— Nary![2]

The incomparable Mark Twain once published a Fourth of July oration he claimed to have intended to deliver—if the previous orator hadn't spoken for so long that there was no time left. According to Twain: "We have a criminal jury system which is superior to any in the world; and its efficacy is only marred by the difficulty of finding twelve men every day who don't know anything and can't read . . . I think I can say, and say with pride, that we have some legislatures that bring higher prices than any in the world."[3]

The Cities Celebrate

The fixed pattern of Fourth of July processions, exercises and dinners was being replaced in the 1850s by more diffuse and lighthearted forms of celebration. The growth of American cities was partly responsible for the change. During the federal period, the leading gentlemen of even the largest American cities could be readily identified and invited to dinner in a large hall. The

A caricature of the bombastic Fourth of July orator and his somnolent audience. (From Mose Skinner, His Centennial Book *by James E. Brown, New England News Co., Boston, 1875)*

gentlemen of a city formed a coherent social group, which quite naturally gathered to celebrate the holiday; and most Americans lived in towns small enough that the entire population formed a single social community.

But by the 1850s, the upper classes of burgeoning cities were far too large to know one another even by name or reputation, and the impulse to gather to celebrate the holiday dissipated accordingly. In a pattern repeated across the nation, large cities like Providence ceased to hold formal Fourth of July exercises, while smaller Rhode Island cities and towns continued the traditional pattern of processions, exercises, orations, dinners and toasts.[4] In major cities, the formal procession was transformed into a lively parade and instead of offering patriotic and politically charged toasts, the citizens entertained themselves with balloon ascensions, regattas, band concerts and steamboat excursions.

New Yorkers looking for Fourth of July entertainment in 1860 could see the sideshow exhibits at Barnum's American Museum or the "Great Living Black Sea Lion" shown by Adam's California Menangerie, which also offered: "SINGING BEARS, CLIMBING BEARS, DANCING BEARS, VAULTING BEARS, BEARS THAT TURN SUMMERSETS." They could view a military parade of 7,000 men as it passed in review before City Hall, watch a regatta off the Battery, or witness official fireworks displays shot off from 11 sites around the city. Those seeking relief from the constant barrage of firecrackers, guns and official fireworks bought passage on the many trains and steamboats leaving for excursions in every direction.[5]

Excursions were a popular Fourth of July entertainment for city folk like the citizens of Norfolk, Virginia, who sailed to watch the fireworks at Old Point Comfort, and those who left Cleveland, Ohio in steamboats bound for towns and picnic groves along the shores of Lake Erie.[6] America was becoming an urban nation and city dwellers whose parents had flocked to formal public exercises now chose to spend their holiday enjoying private excursions. The Sunday school picnics so popular in the 1830s and 40s declined as middle-class families decided to spend the day together, often at picnics in the country.

Every city that had a military company saw it parade on the Fourth of July. Military units were joined by fire companies in their quasi-military uniforms, companies of tradesmen organized according to their craft, and civic organizations, notably the temperance societies. In place of the Revolutionary War veterans, many cities now had marching contingents of veterans of the War of 1812, themselves men in their sixties, and the younger veterans of the Mexican War. In the 1850s, Providence, Rhode Island had a company of 70 men dressed in elegant Continental Army uniforms marching in the Fourth of July parades, an exercise in patriotic nostalgia that is still popular around the nation. Elaborate horse-drawn floats representing such patriotic themes as the "Goddess of Liberty" graced big-city parades, along with such typically Victorian embellish-

A humorous view of the Fourth of July picnic at mid-century, the man in the center has fallen from the swing while a boy hiding behind a log is about to disrupt a courtship by firing a pistol. (The Picnic on the Fourth of July, Engraving by Samuel Hollyer and John Rogers, 1864, after Lilly M. Spencer, Library of Congress)

ments as a floral procession, featuring 100 girls dressed in white and carrying flowers.[7] Some cities organized a single, large parade, but a series of parades by various groups at different times and along routes chosen according to the whim of the organizers was an equally typical pattern.

Any distinguished parade in Boston required the presence of the Ancient and Honorable Artillery Company, a socially elite and lavishly uniformed military company chartered in 1638. The elaborate gaudiness of the military uniforms worn by pre–Civil War militia companies—which were often bright scarlet or blue, encrusted with gold braid, beribboned with contrasting colors, cut in fanciful style, topped by elaborate headgear and tufted with feathers—combined with the elite social status of many companies to make military parades a subject for parody.

None was more widely parodied than the most Ancient and Honorable of them all. High holiday spirits led citizens of several New England cities to dress up in elaborate costumes and march in parody parades styling themselves the Antiques and Horribles or Antics and Intolerables. At Providence in 1858, the Antiques and Horribles included 50 men on horseback, among them Roman knights, Crusaders, Greek Corsairs, Brigands, Harlequins, Falstaff and Richard III. The parody Antiques and Horribles parade spread throughout the nation and continued in many cities until the turn of the century. It is still observed in some New England towns.

Satirical parades also parodied other groups. The Dog Island Fillibusterers marched in Boston in 1858 in parody of politicians and political ideas they disliked, notably women's rights, and the Bourbon Whiskey Reformers turned out to make fun of the temperance-minded Cold Water Armies, ubiquitous at Fourth of July celebrations in the forties and fifties.[8]

Independence Day in a Nation of Nations

The inclination to write satires of Fourth of July orations and mount parody parades, and a public willingness to laugh at them, were signs of national maturity. When the nation was very young, Independence Day was needed to validate our national identity. Making a joke out of such an important holiday would have been frightening—or treasonous—and was therefore unthinkable. By the 1850s Americans were secure enough in their national identity to laugh at their excesses.[9]

The major immigrant groups at mid-century were Irish in the East and Germans in the Midwest; both groups were eager to participate in Fourth of July celebrations. An 1852 Fourth of July parade in New York City included the Shamrock Benevolent Society, Erin Paternal Benevolent Society of Brooklyn,

A boy fires a toy cannon as his brother lights fireworks in honor of the Fourth of July, 1859. (Lithograph by C. H. Brainard, 1859, Library of Congress)

*Boys dart in and out of the crowd setting off firecrackers on the Fourth of July at Portsmouth,
New Hampshire in the early 1850s. (Thomas Bailey Aldrich,* The Story of a Bad Boy, *edition
illustrated by Edwin John Prittie, published by John C. Winston Co., Philadelphia, 1927)*

Hibernian Universal Benevolent Society of New York, Roman Catholic Total Abstinence Society, Irish American Society and Hibernian Benevolent Burial Society. Where there was tension between ethnic groups, the heavy drinking and large crowds of Independence Day celebrations might result in riots, as they did in New York City's Sixth Ward in 1838, when native-born youths engaged in a street fight with Irish immigrants,[10] but it was more usual for immigrants to join other Americans in celebrating the holiday.

In some cities, ethnic communities were among several groups sponsoring Fourth of July festivities and exercises. Charleston, South Carolina had a German parade in 1848, featuring 13 little girls dressed in white, each carrying a white satin flag with the name of a famous person printed on it. Formal exercises at the close of the procession featured an oration in German.[11] At Indianapolis, the Declaration was read in German as well as English, and children from the Irish Catholic Church joined those from Protestant churches at the Sunday school picnic.[12]

Even the best of intentions, however, could not avert all clashes between different cultures. German immigrants were accustomed to the lively Sundays of continental Europe where, after church, the afternoon was an occasion for sports and recreation. American Protestants traditionally regarded Sunday as a Sabbath from all secular activity. Such important events as presidential in-augurations are postponed even today when the date falls on a Sunday, and when the Fourth of July came on Sunday in the 19th century, Independence was celebrated on Saturday or on Monday. Citizens of Indianapolis waxed indignant when, on Sunday, July 4th, 1852, 50 "German infidels" paraded through the city declaring that the Fourth of July was more worthy than the Sabbath.[13] German citizens of Watertown, Minnesota also celebrated Independence Day on Sunday that year, although organizers of the Monday celebration attempted to lure German attendence by featuring orations in both English and German.[14] Many American cities continued to postpone celebration until Monday when the Fourth of July fell on a Sunday until well into the 20th century.

Celebrations on the Westward Trail

Throughout the century, Americans were moving west and thousands of them spent the Fourth of July on the trail. One of the earliest celebrations of Independence Day on the Oregon Trail is recorded not in an archive but in the name of a landmark, Independence Rock. Travelers as early as 1830 already knew this immense stone as Rock Independence, so named by an early party of pioneers who spent the Fourth of July in its shadow.[15]

In 1804, on the first of three Independence Days they would spend on the trail, William Clark and Meriwether Lewis ushered in the day "by a discharge of one shot from our Bow piece," and named a stream near Atchison, Kansas, Independence Creek, a name it still bears. Pioneers journeying overland to Oregon or California were unable to stage parades and fireworks, but they kept the Fourth of July in whatever way they were able. Often, all they were able to do was fire a few celebratory pistol shots at sunrise or add something special to the evening meal at the end of a long day spent moving west,[16] but, in the wistful words of one Ohio-born '49er, "all are talking of how they have spent the Fourth of July heretofore and wondering what is going on in Columbus."[17]

Virtually every wagon train fired a few rounds in honor of Independence, but one party of high-spirited '49ers decided to celebrate with a really loud noise. These patriotic lads dug a hole two-feet deep and in it placed a keg of gunpowder with a slow fuse. From a safe distance, they watched the thing explode with a noise that "seemed to make the neighboring mountains shake."[18]

The Lewis and Clark expedition enjoyed a "sumptuous feast of saddle of venison" on the Fourth of July, and most later traveling parties enjoyed some sort of special meal, but there were parties, notably wagon trains of '49ers, who went much further, arranging elaborate dinners in formal style. These men were willing to lose a day of travel, taking the time to cook and rig prairie banquet halls by fastening tent-flys together, or by lining up two rows of wagons and roofing the aisle between with wagon covers. Formal exercises were held, adhering to all of the established conventions. A President of the Day was elected; some wagon trains even held formal processions. If the party included a minister, he offered a prayer. The Declaration of Independence was read; one of the pioneers delivered an oration; and everyone joined in the singing of the "Star Spangled Banner" and other patriotic songs before sitting down to dinner, which naturally concluded with 13 toasts.[19]

Other travelers, weary from their weeks on the trail, simply took the day off, letting the horses rest and taking advantage of a day without travel to wash clothes, hunt for fresh meat or, in a more traditional observance of the customs of the day, to get drunk.[20] When they reached their destinations in the goldfields of California or the new settlements of the Northwest, pioneers faithfully celebrated Independence Day.

Like citizens of small towns throughout the nation, western pioneers at mid-century continued to celebrate in the traditional manner—within the limitations of their situation. There were few uniformed military companies and fewer marching bands with shiny brass horns to lead the procession, but processions there were. And if there was no local lawyer or politician able to deliver a creditable oration, there were fine orations such as Daniel Webster's famous speech on Adams and Jefferson that a literate pioneer could read aloud. And they could read the Declaration, make 13 or more patriotic toasts and fire a salute—with rifles in lieu of cannon.[21]

A Nation Divides

Back east, verbal Fourth of July volleys were regularly fired by abolitionists whose campaign to win freedom for black as well as white Americans heated up in the 1850s. Growing numbers of northerners found slavery unconscionable and were willing to say so, while southern planters angrily resented northern interference in an institution upon which their fortunes depended. By 1855, when abolitionists and pro-slavery factions fought a small but bitter war in Kansas, feelings in the slaveholding and abolitionist camps ran so high that compromise seemed no longer possible. Northerners insisted that the Union must stand on a foundation of freedom. Southerners, pushed to the wall by abolitionists, were prepared to leave the Union.

Edward Everett was a distinguished elder statesman who had become unpopular by continuing to support the traditional Whig policy of upholding the Union by compromising on slavery. When he was asked to give the Fourth of July Oration at Dorchester, Massachusetts in 1855, the town was posted with abolitionist broadsides protesting the invitation.

O God! what mockery is this!
Our land, how lost to shame!
Well may Europe jeer and hiss
At mention of her name!
For, while she boasts of LIBERTY,
'Neath SLAVERY'S iron sway,
THREE MILLION of her people lie
On Independence Day.

She may not, must not, thus rejoice
Nor of her triumphs tell:
Hushed be the cannon's thundering
And muffled, every bell!
Dissolved in tears, prone in the dust
For mercy let her pray,
That judgement may not on her burst
On Independence Day.

Lo! where her starry banner waves
In many a graceful fold;

There toil and groan and bleed her SLAVES,
And MEN like brutes are sold!
Her hands are red with crimson stains,
And bloody is her way
She wields the lash, she forges chains,
On Independence Day.

Friends of your country—of your race—
Of freedom—and of God
Combine, oppression to efface
And break the tyrant's rod:
All traces of injustice sweep
By moral power away;
Then a glorious jubilee we'll keep
On Independence Day.[22]

The charge was valid. High-flown sentiments on liberty voiced by thousands of orators rang hollow in a nation where one person in every seven was a chattel slave, and speeches praising the Constitution were oddly out of place at a time when freedom of speech and of the press on the subject of slavery were routinely abridged in southern states.

But the abolitionists did not succeed in turning the Fourth of July into an abolitionist holiday. As the nation moved inexorably toward civil war, Independence Day continued to be celebrated North and South. The content of the Fourth of July orations differed; the enthusiasm of the celebration did not.

Notes

1. Thousands of Fourth of July orations were reprinted as pamphlets and are available in libraries. Even more are available in newspapers, which customarily printed in the day's orations later in the week. Works on Fourth of July orations include: Cedric Larson, "Patriotism in Carmine: 162 Years of July 4th Oratory," *Quarterly Journal of Speech*, February, 1940, pp. 12–25; Howard Martin, "The Fourth of July Oration," *Quarterly Journal of Speech*, December 1958, pp. 393–401; Howard H. Martin, "Orations on the Anniversary of American Independence, 1776–1876," Doctoral dissertation, Northwestern University, 1955; Edmund Lester Pearson, "Unfettered Eagles," *Scribner's Monthly*, July, 1924, pp. 61–67; and Henry A. Hawken, *Trumpets of Glory; Fourth of July Orations, 1786–1861*, Salmon Brook Historical Society, Granby, Conn., 1976.

2. Quoted in Barnet Baskerville, "19th Century Burlesque of Oratory," *American Quarterly*, Winter 1968, p. 733.
3. Samuel Clemens, *Mark Twain's Sketches*, Hartford, Conn. 1875, pp. 180–181.
4. *Providence Journal* for the week of July 4th in the 1850s; also, *Chicago Daily Times*, July 3, 1852; and Fletcher M. Green, "Listen to the Eagle Scream: One Hundred Years of the Fourth of July in North Carolina (1776–1876)," *The North Carolina Historical Review*, July, 1954, p. 319; exercises at Bethany College, Ohio, reported in *The Diary of James A. Garfield,* Harry James Brown and Frederick D. Williams, editors, Michigan State University Press, 1967, entry for July 4, 1853; *Down East Diary* by Benjamin Browne Foster, Charles H. Foster, editors, University of Maine at Orono Press, 1975, entry for July 5, 1847 records declining attendance at public exercises at Orono, Maine; *On the Mormon Frontier; The Diary of Hosea Stout, 1844–1861*, Juniata Brooks, editor, University of Utah Press, Salt Lake City, 1964, records the formal exercises held in Deseret; *Diary of Calvin Fletcher*, Gayle Thornbrough, editor, Indiana Historical Society, Indianapolis, 1972, chronicles the formal exercises in Indianapolis, the decline of Sunday School exercises and the increasing diversity of celebrations; and numerous newspaper reports.
5. *New York Times*, Wednesday, July 4, 1860.
6. *Diary of Edmund Ruffin*, William Kauffman Scarborough, editor, Louisiana State University Press, Baton Rouge, 1972, entry for July 5, 1858; *Cleveland Leader* for the 1850s.
7. "Goddess of Liberty" float, *Providence Journal* of Wednesday, July 7, 1858; floral procession from *Down East Diary* by Benjamin Browne Foster, Charles H. Foster, editors, University of Maine at Orono Press, 1975, entry for July 4, 1850; and newspaper accounts.
8. Accounts of parody parades may be found in the *Diary of Calvin Fletcher* entry for July 4, 1859, records presence of "Earth quakes, mountebanks & c," in the Indianapolis parade; *The Journals of Alfred Doten, 1849 to 1903*, Walter Van Tilsburg Clark, editor, University of Nevada Press, Reno, 1973, entry for July 4, 1872, has a detailed account; "The Eighty Second Anniversary of American Independence: Being a Full Report of the Events of the Day in the City of Boston, July 5, 1858," pamphlet in the collection of the Boston Public Library; and newspapers.
9. In addition to Baskerville and Twain, see Lt. George Derby, pseudonym John Phoenix, *Phoenixiania; or, Sketches and Burlesques*, New York, D. Appleton and Company, 1855.
10. *The Diary of Philip Hone, 1828–1851*, Allan Nevins, editor, Dodd, Mead and Co. New York, 1927, entry for July 4, 1838.

11. Robert Pettus Hay, *Freedom's Jubilee: One Hundred Years of the Fourth of July, 1776–1876*, Dissertation, University of Kentucky, 1963, p. 87.

12. *Diary of Calvin Fletcher*, entries for July 4, 1855 and 1856.

13. *Diary of Calvin Fletcher*, entry for July 4, 1852.

14. William F. Whyte, "Chronicles of Early Wisconsin," *The Wisconsin Magazine of History*, 1920–21, pp. 289–290.

15. O.B. Sperlin, "Earliest Celebrations of Independence Day in the Northwest," *The Pacific Northwest Journal*, July, 1944, p. 219.

16. *Diary of Howard Stillwell Stanfield, Overland Trip from Indiana to California in 1864*, Jack Detzler, editor, Indiana University Press, Bloomington, 1969, entry for July 4, 1864; *Overland Days to Montana in 1865, The Diary of Sarah Raymond*, Raymond W. and Mary Lund Settle, editors, Arthur H. Clark Co., Glendale, Calif., 1971, entry for July 4, 1865.

17. *Diaries of Peter Decker; Overland to California in 1849 and Life in the Mines, 1850–1851*, Helen S. Griffen, editor, Talisman Press, Georgetown, California, 1966, entry for July 4, 1849.

18. J.S. Holliday, "On the Gold Rush Trail," *The American West*, July, 1968, p. 38.

19. *Overland to California on the Southwestern Trail, 1849; Diary of Robert Eccleston*, George P. Hammond and Edward H. Howes, editors, University of California Press, Berkeley, 1950; J.S. Holliday, "On the Gold Rush Trail"; and *Gold Rush; The Journals, Drawings, and Other Papers of J. Goldsborough Bruff*, Georgia Willis Read and Ruth Gaines, editors, New York, Columbia University Press, 1944, all entries for July 4th, 1849; Grace Lee Nute, "New Light on Red River History," *Minnesota History Bulletin*, November, 1924, pp. 570–571, July 4, 1862.

20. *Seeking the Elephant, 1849; James Mason Hutchings' Journal of His Overland Trek to California*, Shirley Sargent, editor, Arthur H. Clark, Co. Glendale, California, 1980, entry for July 4, 1849; O.B. Sperlin, "Earliest Celebrations of Independence Day in the Northwest," *The Pacific Northwest Quarterly*, July, 1944, pp. 215–222.

21. Leslie W. Dunlap, "The Oregon Free Press," *The Pacific Northwest Quarterly*, April, 1942, pp. 171–173; "Diary of Rev. Solon W. Mannerly," *Minnesota History*, September, 1928, p. 250; "Minnesota as Seen by Travelers, Isaac I. Stevens and the Pacific Railroad Survey of 1853," *Minnesota History*, June, 1926, p. 140; *Diaries of Peter Decker*, entry for July 4, 1850; James G. Swan, "An Old Time Fourth at Shoalwater Bay," *The American West*, July, 1968, p. 39; *The Journals of Alfred Doten, 1849–1903*.

22. "Fourth of July in Dorchester and Edward Everett," broadside in the collection of the Boston Public Library dated: Dorchester, June 30, 1855.

Civil War 8

On April 15, 1861, one month after he became president, Abraham Lincoln moved to hold the Union together by force, calling up the militia and asking for a special session of Congress to convene on the Fourth of July.

South Carolina seceded upon receiving news of Abraham Lincoln's election in December 1860. Six states of the lower South, Mississippi, Florida, Alabama, Georgia, Louisiana and Texas, had followed South Carolina by early February. Eight slave states remained in the Union, hoping that the Union could be preserved but unwilling to see force used against the seceding states.

As spring came in 1861, men of peace worked earnestly but without success to find a formula that could prevent war. President Lincoln, who took office on March 4, 1861, struggled to hold the Union together without bloodshed.

Most federal arsenals and forts located in the Deep South had been seized by seceding states in the winter of 1860–1861, but Fort Sumter in Charleston Harbor was still held by a small Union garrison. By April, that garrison was almost out of food. Lincoln, working to stave off war and hold the loyal slave states in the Union, proposed to send in a resupply ship carrying only food. On April 12, 1861, South Carolina, rejecting Lincoln's bid to prevent war from starting at Fort Sumter, opened fire. The Union garrison surrendered on the afternoon of the following day.

News of the fighting at Ft. Sumter drove Virginia, Arkansas, Tennessee and North Carolina into the Confederacy and galvanized the North to come to the defense of the Union. Two days after Sumter fell, President Lincoln called for 75,000 three-month volunteers, and yet it was not entirely clear at the time that the North would go to war.

The Test of the Union

As a young Louisiana woman wrote in her diary that July Fourth, "Congress meets today. The lives of thousands hang on its decision. Will it be for peace or war?"[1] Southerners hoped that Northern rhetoric about saving the Union might prove hollow. Rather than fight a war, perhaps when Congress met it would let the Confederacy secede unopposed, an option known as peaceable disunion. There were Northerners who judged such a course preferable to war, and Southerners who did not believe that men would actually fight and die to defend an abstraction like Union; these and others awaited word from Washington that Congress had decided against war.

Such Congressional passivity would have been a grave dissappointment to the many Southern men looking forward to military glory in what they expected would be a short march to victory, and to an equal number of Northern men rushing to enlist before the short, glorious war ended in Union victory without them. Wiser heads passed Independence Day with fearful foreboding.

Southern secessionists believed that in leaving the Union they were doing no more but no less than the Founding Fathers had done in declaring independence from Great Britain in 1776, but they differed on what their attitude toward that earlier declaration of independence should now be. Many agreed with the Charleston, South Carolina editor who wrote, "We are fighting as our fathers fought . . . for the cardinal and essential elements of self-government and independence," and celebrated Independence Day as they had always done— except that the canon boomed 11 salutes, one for each seceding state, in place of the national salute of 34.[2] A Wilmington, North Carolina editor took the opposite position, refusing to celebrate on the grounds that the Fourth of July "belongs to the history of a nation which no longer exists."[3] Some Southern individuals and cities observed the Fourth of July 1861 enthusiastically, while others self-consciously abstained. But all trained their eyes on Washington, awaiting the next move.

In Northern cities the day was celebrated with the usual festivities, except that the troops passing in review were en route to Washington and the fashionable destinations for picnic excursions were the training grounds of regiments awaiting orders to move south. But the nation's attention was not focused on the glories of the Revolution. North and South, Americans read dispatches about skirmishing in the border states and waited to hear what Congress would do.

Congress convened on the Fourth of July and promptly ended any lingering doubts about Northern resolve by authorizing President Lincoln to recruit half a million men for the duration of the war. Blue and gray armies marched off with all the enthusiasm of men who have never known the reality of war. Within three weeks, hundreds of soldiers lay dead at Bull Run and the nation was shocked into the realization that it was committed to a bloody struggle.

The Fourth of July was not celebrated again by the Confederacy. There were gestures of respect for the anniversary of the first American Revolution: newspapers printed editorials about liberty and the twin revolutions of 1776 and 1861, many cities fired 11-gun Confederate salutes, some stores closed and slaves were given a holiday on many plantations. But Southerners were in no mood to celebrate the Independence of the United States of America while half of that nation fought to deny independence to the other half.[4]

Northerners kept the holiday in traditional if subdued style with fireworks, military parades, excursions to the country and formal exercises in the towns, all tinged with an overriding interest in the war. Fourth of July editorials called on the memory of Washington's glorious deeds to encourage enlistment; orators spoke on the progress of the war; choruses sang Union marching songs; and a minister invited to offer the invocation at Fourth of July exercises intoned, "God bless our native country! she is warring for the right ..."[5]

Eleven states had seceded from the Union, 24 remained, including four slave states and the newly formed West Virginia, which seceded from Virginia to stay with the Union, but opinion was not neatly divided by state. There were Union sympathizers throughout the South, especially in the border states. The wrenching task of deciding whether to secede or stay in the Union had sundered the political fabric and torn men's souls, especially in the border states. A Southern peace movement grew as the war dragged on after Gettysburg. Nor was the North unified in its decision to fight for the Union.

Many Northerners, even many who conceded that slavery was morally repugnant, believed in the right of a state to make its own laws, and to leave the Union if it chose. Southern sympathizers, known as Copperheads, formed a powerful political force made more influential by widespread discontent when the war went badly for the North—as it did most of the time. Month after month the high casualty figures were unrequited by territorial gains.

Northern armies, raw recruits commanded by inexperienced officers, faced the task of conquering, mile by stubbornly defended mile, a large and hostile enemy territory. An army defending its homeland is always at an advantage; to win the war, the South needed only to defend its borders until the Union grew weary of fighting. The North had more factories, more farms, better transportation and more men, but after the first volunteer regiments marched off, the men were more or less reluctant enlistees from a country that began to tire of war almost as soon as it began. The prosperity of farmers throughout the northern plains was threatened by the Southern grip on the Mississippi. As long as the Confederacy held the river, western farmers had no outlet for their crops. But it was the casualty lists and the unceasing demand for more soldiers that killed enthusiasm for the Union cause.

Independence Day on the Battlefields of Gettysburg and Vicksburg

By the Fourth of July, 1863 there were no troops at all to parade in northeastern cities; even the elderly Home Guards had been rushed to Pennsylvania to stand against Lee and the Army of Virginia as they marched north, threatening to encircle Washington. Lee's army crossed the Potomac on June 17. On July 1, the Army of Virginia met the Army of the Potomac near the small town of Gettysburg and fighting began. On the Fourth of July, an anxious nation awaited word of the outcome of the greatest battle of the war. Early on the afternoon of July third, Lee ordered Longstreet's three divisions, under Pickett, Pettigrew and Trimble, to attack the Union center and Pickett's gallant men began their famous charge across open fields that sloped gently upward to the ridge of Cemetery Hill and the last real chance for a military victory that could win Confederate independence.

In the West, General Grant's nine-month campaign to capture Vicksburg and wrest the Mississippi from Confederate control culminated in a siege that was already in its sixth week on Independence Day. Telegraph lines had long since been cut in the heavy fighting that raged through the Mississippi valley, but Northerners eagerly read three- and four-day-old dispatches that brought news from Vicksburg. General Grant himself knew that the two armies had met in Pennsylvania, but would not know how the struggle ended until the fighting had been over for three days. Simultaneous victories at Gettysburg and Vicksburg would decide the outcome of the war: if the South won at Gettysburg and held Vicksburg, the Northern peace element would be sufficiently strengthened to push for an end to hostilities. Southern loss of the Mississippi, and with it the western Confederacy, would fatally weaken the Southern cause. On the anniversary of its birth, the nation awaited news of its fate.

At 10:30 A.M. on Independence Day, President Lincoln issued a message from the White House and the nation's telegraph wires hummed with his confident assurance of victory at Gettysburg. Yet, all day long on the Fourth of July, two armies faced each other on the bloody fields of Pennsylvania wheat— not fighting, yet not retreating. Crowds gathered at newspaper offices where the latest dispatches from Gettysburg and Washington were posted. The appalling scale of the carnage was made dramatically clear by steadily lengthening casualty lists, but along with an understanding of the high price that had been paid, came the realization that the Union Army had turned back the Southern invasion. No further word of fighting came over the tense wires. On the fourth day, the great battle was over. News came that Lee was retreating and, as night fell on the Fourth of July, the North was swept with a thrill of relief and exhilaration. The threat of invasion was ended. The tide had turned on Independence Day.

At Vicksburg, General Pemberton, a Philadelphian fighting for the Confederacy in a war that was an ideological as it was regional, spent July third considering his options. Grant had surrounded the apparently impregnable city in a long and brilliant campaign. After a six-week siege, the 30,000 defenders were low on supplies.

Pemberton knew from his spies that transporting 30,000 prisoners would severly strain Northern resources and, solicitous for the well-being of his men, hoped to arrange terms that would allow them to be paroled instead of being imprisoned. Parole was a common recourse of both armies in the Civil War. Surrendering troops were required to sign pledges that they would not return to the fighting. It was advantageous to the capturing army, which saved the expense of maintaining prisoners, and the parolees sowed dissatisfaction in their home region.

Pemberton calculated that Union eagerness to obtain a surrender on the Fourth of July would enable him to arrange more liberal terms on that day than on any other. Therefore, white flags appeared over Vicksburg on the eve of Independence Day, and Pemberton came out to parley. General U.S. Grant, nicknamed "Unconditional Surrender" by his men, at first replied that he would accept only surrender without terms, which he would be able to exact within a few days in any case, but negotiations continued and Grant reconsidered.

Grant knew Pemberton's men to be predominately from the Southwest and likely, if paroled, to stay at home in states that would now be cut off from the Confederacy. Returning the others to homes within the effective Confederacy might actually help the Union cause: the sight of able-bodied men waving their parole papers under the noses of Confederate draft boards scraping the barrel for old men and boys to put into uniform would be demoralizing for the South. More compellingly, Grant lacked transportation. General Pemberton's intelligence reports had been accurate. Grant might have insisted on unconditional surrender only to end by paroling the Confederate prisoners in order to free his boats to transport Union troops for an attack on Port Hudson, the final Confederate stronghold on the Mississippi. Port Hudson surrendered soon after learning of the fall of Vicksburg, opening the Mississippi to transport the commerce of the Northwest and weakening the antiwar movement in that part of the Union.

Grant's choice was between a Fourth of July surrender with parole or an unconditional surrender within a few days. As he made his decision, Grant knew of the fighting in Pennsylvania and knew also that Southern victory at Gettysburg would cause panic throughout the North. Judging correctly that a Fourth of July victory would be symbolically important to the Union, Grant accepted Pemberton's terms.[6] On the Fourth of July, 1863, the Confederate garrison at Vicksburg surrendered.

Couriers bringing news of the fall of Vicksburg reached Cairo, Illinois on July 7. Telegraph operators at Cairo sent word of Grant's triumph speeding through the nation, which rejoiced over news of the most glorious Fourth of July since 1776. Church bells rang, 34 gun national salutes boomed from cannon and crowds cheered in the streets. The relief that flooded the North when Lee retreated from Gettysburg, dampened by knowledge of heavy casualties, ripened into exultation at word of the fall of Vicksburg. Two great victories on Independence Day were interpreted as a clear indication of divine favor and Northerners confidently expected to celebrate the Fourth of July, 1864, in a reunified nation.

The Slow March to Victory

Lincoln's Emancipation Proclamation became effective on January 1, 1863, making the Independence Days of 1863 and 1864 true celebrations of freedom. Ten thousand freedmen paraded through the streets of Louisville on the Fourth of July 1863, and the black citizens of Baltimore met on July Fourth in 1864 to present President Lincoln with a Bible as an expression of their appreciation.[7] But the most symbolically satisfying black celebration of the war years took place on the banks of the Mississippi.

At seven A.M. on the Fourth of July 1864, a gay party of freedmen and Northern teachers gathered on the levee at Vicksburg to board a small ship that would take them on a three-hour cruise to Davis' Bend, the penninsula where Jefferson Davis' home and plantation stood, empty, while the president of the Confederacy and his family lived in Richmond, the Southern capital. The doors of the Davis mansion, hung with garlands woven of evergreen and flowers, opened to welcome the former slaves. There were formal exercises, a dinner with 13 toasts and songs culminating in a solo by a teenager who had recently crossed Union lines to freedom:

An artist accompanying the Union Army drew this picture of the Fourth of July surrender of Vicksburg. General Pemberton stands on the hilltop, surveying his troops as they march out and stack arms. General Grant and his staff ride up from the left. (Harper's Weekly, August 1, 1863, p. 489)

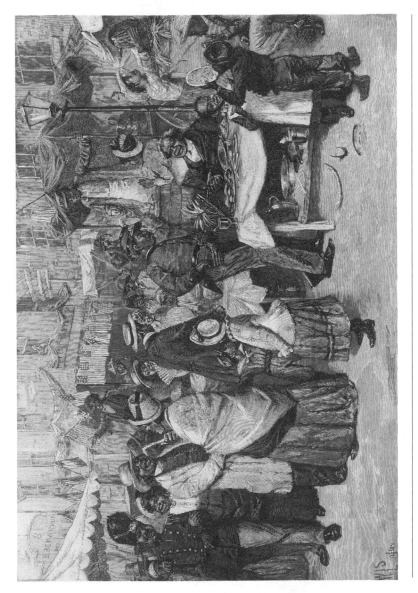

Freedmen celebrating the Fourth of July. (Harper's Weekly. July 7, 1888, p. 488)

We heard the proclamation, master hush it as he will:
The bird, he sang it to us, hopping on the cotton-hill;
Father Abraham has spoken, and the message has been sent;
The prison-doors he opened, and out the prisoners went.
They said, "Now colored brethren, you shall be forever free,
From the first of January, eighteen hundred sixty-three."[8]

Independence Day 1864 in the North was the most subdued Fourth of a war that had gone on too long. The end was in sight, yet getting there was painful, bloody and slow. Northerners had hoped to capture Richmond by the Fourth of July; instead, newspapers printed the names of men fallen in heavy fighting around Petersburg, 20 miles from Richmond, where the armies of Grant and Lee faced each other across trenches for nine terrible months. Not until April 9, 1865, did General Robert E. Lee surrender to General Ulysses S. Grant at the little town of Appomattox Courthouse, and the North rejoiced in its hard-won victory.

The Union Forever

The Fourth of July 1865 was celebrated throughout the North with more enthusiasm than any holiday in living memory. Schools and businesses closed early on the third, giving eager Americans a head start on the great day. Regiments on their way home were understandably reluctant to pause for Fourth of July parades, which were conspicuously short of troops but replete with everything else: marching bands, fire departments, columns of schoolchildren, floats carrying young girls dressed in white, one girl for each state in the Union, societies of tradesmen, fraternal organizations, floats representing the goddesses of liberty and peace and, in Virginia City, Nevada, a mounted troop of Indians wearing peace-paint.[9]

American representatives in Europe, who had endured four years of European sympathy for the Confederacy and the presence of a sizable community of Copperheads, celebrated gleefully.[10] Admiral and Mrs. Farragut were guests of honor at the great celebration in Boston, while General Grant himself attended the celebration at Albany, where he presented the battle flags of 200 New York regiments to Governor Fenton. The year 1865 also saw the cornerstone laid for the Soldier's Monument at Gettysburg. The dedication of war memorials would be a feature of Fourth of July observances for many years to come.

Whites in the South who had supported the Confederacy saw little reason to celebrate in the years just after the war, but Southern blacks celebrated their new freedom joyously. Public picnics, parades, dances and formal exercises were

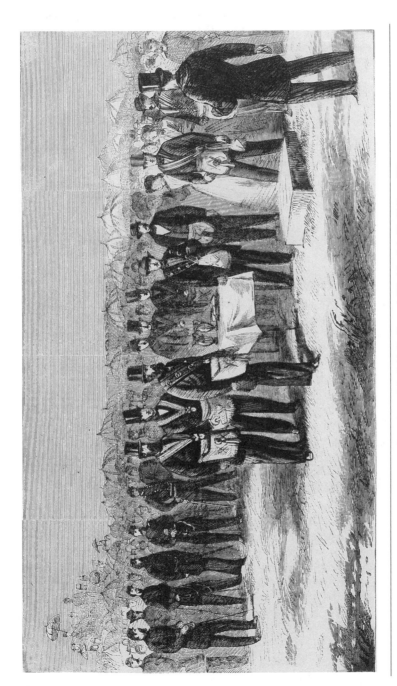

Laying the cornerstone of the Soldier's Monument at Gettysburg, July 4, 1865. (Harper's Weekly, July 22, 1865, p. 453)

held throughout the South in large cities and small towns by black citizens. Not until Reconstruction was over and blacks had again been subordinated by their former owners would Southern whites hold public Fourth of July celebrations.[11]

Notes

1. *Brokenburn; the Journal of Kate Stone, 1861–1868*, John Q. Anderson, editor, Louisiana State University Press, Baton Rouge, 1955, entry for July 4, 1861.

2. Robert Pettus Hay, "Freedom's Jubilee: One Hundred Years of the Fourth of July, 1776–1876," dissertation, University of Kentucky, 1967, pp. 256–259; *Diary of Miss Emma Holmes, 1861–1866*, John F. Marszalek, editor, Louisiana State University Press, Baton Rouge, 1979, entry for July 4, 1861.

3. Fletcher M. Green, "Listen to the Eagle Scream," *North Carolina Historical Review*, July, 1954, p. 535.

4. *Diary of Edmund Ruffin*, William Kauffman Scarborough, editor, Louisiana State University Press, Baton Rouge, 1972, entry for July 4, 1862; *Diary of Miss Emma Holmes*; Brokenburn; *The Journal of Kate Stone*; Hay, *Freedom's Jubilee*; Green, *Listen to the Eagle Scream*.

5. Northern newspapers and broadsides; quotation is from *Songs for the Fourth of July Celebration, 1862*, J.E. Farwell & Co., Printers to the City, Boston, pamphlet in the collection of the American Antiquarian Society, Worcester, Mass.

6. Bruce Catton, *Grant Moves South*, Little, Brown, and Co., Boston, 1960, pp. 471–487; Col. J. F. Fuller, *The Generalship of Ulysses S. Grant*, John Murray, London, 1929, p. 157.

7. Leonard Sweet, "The Fourth of July and Black Americans in the Nineteenth Century," *Journal of Negro History*, July, 1976, p. 272.

8. William Wells Brown, *The Negro in the American Rebellion; His Heroism and His Fidelity*, A. G. Brown & Co., Boston, 1880, pp. 298–308, the lyric quoted appears in dialect.

9. Northern newspapers; Indians appeared in Virginia City parade, *The Journals of Alfred Doten, 1849–1903*, Walter Van Tilburg Clark, editor, University of Nevada Press, Reno, 1973, entry for July 4, 1865.

10. John Bigelow, *Retrospections of an Active Life*, Volume III, 1865–1866, Baker & Taylor, New York, 1909, pp. 90–111.

11. Newspapers; *Mary Chestnut's Civil War*, C. Vann Woodward, editor, Yale University Press, New Haven, 1981, entry for "Black 4th of July— 1865"; Green, "Listen to the Eagle Scream," pp. 538–541; Sweet, "The

Fourth of July and Black Americans in the Nineteenth Century," p. 273; and Hay, *Freedom's Jubilee*, pp. 266–273.

Centennial 9

As darkness fell on December 31, 1875, thousands of Philadelphians gathered outside Independence Hall to welcome the new year at the spot where the courageous members of the Continental Congress had declared Independence 100 years before. Shortly before midnight, Mayor Stokley made a short speech to a crowd that packed every inch of street and sidewalk in Independence Square, spilled over into surrounding streets and perched in windows and atop walls. Then, as the clock struck midnight, the mayor hoisted to the top of a flagpole a replica of the flag raised by George Washington on Cambridge Common on January 1, 1776. Pandemonium broke loose.

A band playing the "Star Spangled Banner" could scarcely be heard above the din of firecrackers and pistols. Every church bell in the city rang out, every factory and train whistle blew, every bell in schoolhouse or workshop pealed, and every noisemaking instrument played to welcome the centennial year. As noise resounded through the city, fireworks streaked skyward over Independence Square. The effect, even in quiet districts at the edge of the city, was remarkable, "seeming as if some terrible disaster were occurring, such as the sacking of a city, and the sound of a vast multitude wailing and shrieking at a distance."[1]

A Fair Way to Celebrate 100 Years

Discussion of the proper way to celebrate the Centennial began years in advance. Following the tremendous success of the 1851 Great Exhibition at London's Crystal Palace, international fairs became the fashion and it quite naturally occurred to many individuals that a centennial exhibition would be a fitting way to celebrate.[2] Everyone had an opinion about where the exhibition should be held—New York, Washington and Boston were proposed—and whether the exhibition should be held at all. Some thought that the condition of the nation did not offer much to celebrate; others believed that it would cost too much money; still others expended great energy debating such issues as whether monarchies should be invited to participate in an exposition celebrating the birth of a republic.

All of this debate presumed that there would be an exhibition, although that was by no means a foregone conclusion. All that was clear at the outset was that an exhibition required a great deal of money—$10,000,000, the cost of the recent exhibition at Vienna, was accepted as a reasonable estimate—and the parsimonious federal government of the era was unlikely to lay out a cent.

That a centennial exhibition took place, and was a smashing success, was due to the initiative of the citizens of Philadelphia. In January of 1870, the Philadelphia Select Council resolved to endorse an International Centennial Exhibition. The city granted the use of 450 acres in Fairmount Park to the private corporation planning the exhibition. Congressman Daniel Morrell of Pennsylvania managed to get a bill through Congress endorsing the exhibition, although congressional attitudes were revealed in the specification that the United States government would not be liable for any expenses incurred.

It was the difficult job of the Centennial Commission to raise money from a skeptical nation for a fair that many viewed as extravagant, impractical and doomed to failure. Yet the effort went forward and, with nearly all of the money coming from Pennsylvania and Philadelphia itself, ground was broken for the first exhibit hall on July 4, 1874. Not until March 1875, with plans for buildings and exhibits already made public by many foreign governments, was Congress finally embarrassed into appropriating half a million dollars for a United States government building.

Beginning in 1874, and at an ever-increasing pace in 1875 and the winter of 1876, visitors to Fairmont Park could watch an immense enterprise take shape. Two rail spurs were built to the site on which five huge buildings and numerous smaller ones rose. Main Hall, reputedly the largest building in the world, faced Machinery Hall, housing the world's largest engine, across the Grand Plaza. Nearby Horticulture Hall, a giant greenhouse, and the huge bulk of Memorial and Agriculture Halls, encrusted with tiers of Victorian architectural embellishment, were being prepared for the millions of visitors whom the Commissioners hoped would come.

Yet the nation remained indifferent or cynically certain that the vast enterprise would never open. In January 1876, with freight trains daily unloading crated exhibits from around the nation and the world, it appeared that the cynics might be correct. All private fund-raising efforts were insufficient; it looked as though the exhibition would indeed fail unless Congress could be persuaded to offer some financial backing. In a close vote opposed by many western and nearly all of the recently returned white southern Democrats, a bill passed authorizing a loan of one-and-a-half million dollars to the Centennial Commission.

Scandals in the Centennial Year

Congress was preoccupied with other matters in the centennial year. Beginning with the revelations of the liquor tax-evasion racket known as the Whiskey Ring, the Grant administration was rocked by a series of scandals revealing corrupt practices at every level of the federal government from the Cabinet and the president's personal aides down. Worse was yet to come, for the presidential election of 1876 was the most fraudulent election in American history.

Governor Rutherford B. Hayes of Ohio ran on the Republican ticket against Democratic Governor Samuel J. Tilden of New York. Strong-arm tactics to get out a favorable vote, practiced by both sides, were especially egregious in the South. Federal troops sent after the war to keep order and ensure the rights of freed slaves had been withdrawn from all but three southern states—Florida, Louisiana and South Carolina. Throughout the South white Democrats and the Ku Klux Klan worked effectively to ensure that black citizens did not dare exercise their new right to vote. When it became clear on election night that Tilden would win unless Florida, Louisiana and South Carolina all went for Hayes, a struggle began, which included fraudulently invalidated votes, bribery and outright falsification of vote counts.

Who won depends on who was counting. If all southern blacks had voted freely, their votes would have been sufficient to give South Carolina, Louisiana and Mississippi, and with them the election, to Hayes—but blacks did not vote freely. Many did not vote at all; others were intimidated into voting the Democratic ticket.

A fair count of the ballots actually cast would have given the election to Tilden, but the count was anything but fair. Whether it is worse to steal an election by denying the vote to certain citizens as the Democrats did, or with false counts by dishonestly partisan election officials, as the Republicans did, is an open question. In 1876 Hayes became president and democracy lost.

Most Americans in the centennial year thought even less of the rights of Indians than they did of the rights of blacks. A relentless if irregular policy pushed the Indians into smaller and smaller pieces of territory, and provided for the hunting down and killing of those who chose to fight for their land. News of one of the most famous Indian battles reached the nation on July 5, 1876, when telegraph lines out of Fort Lincoln, Dakota Territory hummed with the news that Lt. Col. George Custer, a popular hero of the Civil and Indian wars, had been killed with his entire command at Little Bighorn.

The Centennial Theme and a New State

Election fraud, military disaster and revelation of the worst scandals of the Grant administration were still in the future on New Year's Eve. Not only in Philadelphia, but throughout the nation, Americans gathered to celebrate the Centennial. The year was welcomed with fireworks, parades, church services, speeches and feasting by a people who felt they had a great deal to celebrate. Only the South, where poverty and the destruction of war were stark facts of life, failed to participate in the Centennial enthusiasm.

The Centennial seemed to be everywhere. Advertisers promoted everything from Centennial books to Centennial stockings—striped red, white and blue. Patriots could eat from Centennial dishes, wear Centennial neckties and smoke Centennial cigars. The event lent color to every aspect of American life.

Phineas T. Barnum went on the road with a Centennial edition of his circus. Every performance of the year began with a 13-gun salute from a battery of cannon, there was a chorus of hundreds to sing the "Star Spangled Banner," a live eagle, performers dressed in "Revolutionary" style costumes and fireworks every night.[3]

The Centennial theme was put to serious uses as well. Calling an event "Centennial" could add lustre to an already important enterprise, as was the case when Fisk University dedicated a new building on the Centennial New Year's Day,[4] or it could inspire people to undertake a project that needed attention in any case, as happened when the citizens of Alburgh, Vermont spent several Centennial days in June raking, planting new trees and building a fence around the common.[5]

The biggest Centennial project was the admission of Colorado to the Union, earning it the nickname Centennial State.

The criteria for admitting territories as states were imprecise. Some states were rushed in for a variety of political reasons, others had to knock patiently at the door of Congress for years. Some were heavily settled and developed at admission; others were virtual wildernesses with a few large towns and a narrow strip of settled territory. Colorado at the time of its admission comformed to this latter model. There were a few cities, farms, and mining communities in a settled belt stretching from Fort Collins to Colorado Springs, surrounded by thousands of acres of uncharted wilderness. The population was only sufficient to justify a single member of the United States House of Representatives, plus the requisite two senators, but that translated into three votes in the Electoral College and the people of Colorado could be counted on to vote the Republican ticket.

In March of 1875, with an eye on the upcoming presidential election, the Republican majority in the House passed legislation enabling Colorado to enter the Union. A state constitution was completed in March, and ratified just in time for a gala Fourth of July celebration honoring both statehood and the Centennial.

The Exhibition Is On

Centennial events were held across the nation, but national attention focused increasingly on Philadelphia, as the scale and likely success of the International Centennial Exhibition became clear. The perennial American appetite for royal visits was whetted by an announcement that Emperor Dom Pedro of Brazil had accepted an invitation to attend the opening of the exhibition. Disapproval of the irresponsible behavior of Edward, prince of Wales, who had been invited to attend but who chose to go tiger hunting in India instead, could not dampen enthusiasm for the royal guest. Dom Pedro was only the second crowned head of state to set foot on American soil (King Kalakaua of Hawaii was the first), and he was welcomed with an effusive outpouring odd in a nation celebrating the 100th anniversary of the overthrow of a monarch in favor of a republican government.

On May 10, 1876, a crowd of 180,000 poured onto the grounds of the Centennial Exhibition to witness the official opening by President Grant, Dom Pedro and a host of dignitaries.[6] The exhibition was America's chance to show off its culture and its industrial progress. The halls of the exhibition were filled with mechanical marvels and the products of field and mine. But the Centennial was also a coming-of-age party for a nation that suffered from a cultural inferiority complex and felt a strong need to demonstrate to itself and to Europe that Americans not only knew how to make machines and money, but knew how to produce and appreciate culture.

To this end, John Greenleaf Whittier was persuaded to write a hymn for the opening ceremonies. Other poems were commissioned, as was music by American composers and a "Centennial March" by Richard Wagner, which is not among his more highly regarded efforts. Memorial Hall, filled with paintings and sculpture loaned by European governments and works produced by American artists, was one of the most popular buildings on the grounds. The presence of so many European works, even though Europe did not send its finest art, was exciting at a time when the great American museums were not yet established and few Americans had the opportunity to travel in Europe. A few works of art were commissioned for the exhibition, notably Edmonia Lewis' sculpture "Death of Cleopatra," and a prize in painting went to Edward M. Bannister's "Under the Oaks." These were two of the few contributions to the Centennial by black Americans who, for the most part, were carefully excluded from participation.[7] The most popular work of art to emerge from the exhibition was Archibald Willard's "Spirit of '76," which drew large crowds and embarked on a national tour after the exhibition closed.

Music fairly flooded the exhibition. There were regularly scheduled and special concerts by bands, orchestras and smaller ensembles, as well as recitals on the Centennial Organ, with nearly 3,000 pipes, housed in the eastern gallery of the Main Building. Pianos were omnipresent at the exhibition, as they were in Victorian America. Every home with pretentions to middle-class status had a piano in the parlor, and every young lady played, or spent years of her life attempting to learn. Every piano manufacturer in America exhibited instruments at the Centennial, offering such frequent recitals in contiguous exhibit space that the Centennial Commission had to impose a recital schedule to restore harmony.

The exhibition had displays of George Washington's false teeth and Daniel Webster's plow. There was needlework stitched by Queen Victoria herself. The hand and torch of the Statue of Liberty were put on display by the committee working to raise funds to build a pedestal in New York harbor to hold the colossal sculpture. A Japanese house was assembled on the grounds under the eyes of spectators, who marveled to see that no nails were used. The Catholic Total Abstinence Society offered pure water from a gargantuan fountain, topped by a statue of Moses towering above Lafayette, Pulaski, DeGrasse and other brave officers who aided the American cause and were undeniably Catholic even if they were not teetotalers.

But machines were the marvels of the age and industry was the soul of the exhibition. Backers hoped that it would promote the sale of American manufactures abroad and exhibitors came to advertise their wares. The public came to gaze upon the wonders of technology. The giant Corliss engine, largest in the world, powered displays in Machinery Hall. Here visitors could purchase fine silk handkerchiefs made from fabric woven before their eyes, watch printing presses run off that day's edition of the New York *Herald, Sun,* or *Times,* and

President Grant and Dom Pedro of Brazil start the giant Corliss Engine to open the International Centennial Exhibition. (Harper's Weekly, May 27, 1876, p. 424)

see a small girl operate a machine that every day inserted 180,000 pins into paper cards.

The latest technological innovations were on display. Visitors were awed by the immense size of the new cannon shown by Krupp of Germany and intrigued by "an engine from the same country which works by gas, the gas is mixed with air in the cylinder, then exploded, which forces the piston upwards, the explosion produces a vacuum and the air forces the piston downwards."[8] A newly invented typewriting machine was very popular, but little notice was taken of an invention called the telephone displayed by Alexander Graham Bell.

The exhibition grew in popularity as visitors' reports spread through the nation. Attendance was light in the early weeks and through the hot summer months when the exhibition's asphalt roads, a marvel to Americans accustomed only to dirt roads and uneven wooden paving blocks, turned to sticky goo, but by early fall crowds of over 100,000 a day were surging through the turnstiles. It seemed that the entire country was bent on visiting the great fair. The Centennial Exhibition mounted by Philadelphia in the face of national indifference had become *the* event of the centennial year.

An Old-Fashioned Fourth of July

Cannon thundered across the nation at sunrise on the centennial Fourth of July, announcing a national intention to celebrate. Independence Day had declined as a public celebration and was eclipsed by Decoration Day, forerunner of Memorial Day. The Civil War was a fresh scar on the body politic and Decoration Day was the holiday Americans would celebrate with parades and orations for as long as there were veterans of the Grand Army of the Republic able to line up, march down Main Street, and lay a wreath in honor of their fallen comrades. In honor of the Centennial, however, Americans were resolved to have an old-fashioned Fourth of July.

The citizens of Canton, Connecticut, the American community at Canton, China and just about every American city, town or community in between put on the kind of formal Fourth of July exercises that had been falling into disfavor for 20 years.[9] There were hymns, prayers, songs, patriotic odes and patriotic orations. There were readings of the Declaration of Independence and historical addresses. There were 13-gun salutes at sunrise and 38-gun salutes at noon, a volley for each state, including Colorado. Bells rang, bands played, fireworks lit up the sky, and on every Main Street there was a parade. There were celebrations wherever there were Americans, but on the Centennial Fourth the attention of the nation focused on Philadelphia, where the epochal document was written and signed.

Fireworks light the sky over Union Square in New York City on the Centennial Fourth. (Harper's Weekly, July 22, 1876, p. 596)

Independence Hall is illuminated at midnight on the Fourth of July 1876, as fireworks burst over the heads of the crowd. (Harper's Weekly, July 22, 1876, p. 593)

Richard Henry Lee of Virginia reads the Declaration of Independence at Independence Square on July, 4, 1876. (Frank Leslie's Illustrated Newspaper, *July 22, 1876*)

Philadelphia welcomed the nation's second century where it had greeted the first, at Independence Hall. Stores and businesses throughout the city were closed for five days, beginning on Saturday, July 1, when the first of a series of celebratory events planned for the city by the Centennial Commission was held. By Monday night, the people of Philadelphia were at a pitch of excitement. A torchlight parade wound through the city streets toward Independence Square, where tens of thousands of visitors had joined Phialdelphians to celebrate the great anniversary. At midnight, the new Liberty Bell—made from four Civil War cannon and hung in the tower of Independence Hall to replace the original bell, which had cracked—rang 13 times and the city repeated the noisy welcome it had given the New Year.

Exercises in Philadelphia on the morning of the Fourth were planned as a celebration of both Independence and the reconciliation of the Union. The Commissioners went to great lengths to invite southern military companies to parade and southern dignitaries to sit on the reviewing stand outside Independence Hall. There was general criticism of President Grant for declining to attend the ceremony, although a glittering array of generals, highnesses, excellencies and honorables did attend. The highlight of the program came when Richard Henry Lee of Virginia, grandson and namesake of the Virginia delegate who brought the resolution on "Independency" from the Virginia Convention to the Continental Congress, read the Declaration of Independence.

Just as Mr. Lee finished reading, five women who had been denied permission to participate in the official program rose from the section of the hall reserved for members of the press and proceeded up the aisle. Upon reaching the podium, the redoubtable Susan B. Anthony presented a copy of the "Woman's Declaration of Rights" to the startled master of ceremonies, Senator Thomas Ferry. He accepted it with a bow and watched the five women retreat down the aisle distributing copies of their declaration, while General Joseph Hawley shouted "Order, order."[10] As Thomas Jefferson himself once said, "a little rebellion, now and then, is a good thing."[11]

Notes

1. William Randel, "John Lewis Reports the Centennial," *Pennsylvania Magazine*, 1955, p. 367; and newspapers.

2. Faith Pizor, "Preparations for the Centennial Exhibition of 1876," *Pennsylvania Magazine of History and Biography,"* April, 1970, pp. 213–231; *William Pierce Randel, Centennial; American Life in 1876*, Chilton Book Co., Phila., 1969; Dee Brown, *The Year of the Century: 1876*, Charles Scribner's Sons, New York, 1966.

3. Randel, *Centennial*, pp. 327–328.
4. *Harper's Weekly*, Jan. 1, 1776.
5. Homer L. Calkin, "Vermont and the Centennial of American Independence, 1876," *Vermont History*, Fall, 1975, p. 255.
6. Contemporary newspapers and magazines covered the Centennial Exhibition extensively. It is documented in the books by Randel and Brown cited above and in Homer Calkin, "Music During the Centennial," *The Pennsylvania Magazine of History and Biography*, July, 1976, pp. 374–389; William H. Crew, "Centennial Notes," *Pennsylvania Magazine of History and Biography*, July 1976, pp. 406–413; Randel, "John Lewis Reports the Centennial," July, 1955, pp. 364–367; Philip S. Foner, "Black Participation in the Centennial of 1876," *Phylon*, Winter, 1978, pp. 283–296; David Bailey, *Eastward Ho!, or Leaves from the Diary of a Centennial Pilgrim*, Highland, Ohio, 1877; John S. Ingram, *The Centennial Exhibiton Described and Illustrated*, Hubbard, Philadelphia, 1877; John D. McCabe, *The Illustrated History of the Centennial Exhibition*, National Publishing Co., Philadelphia, 1876; Christine Hunter Davidson, "The Centennial of 1876: The Exposition, and Culture for America," dissertation, Yale University, 1948; "Characteristics of the International Fair," *Atlantic Monthly*, July, 1876, pp. 85–91; William Dean Howells, "At the Centennial," *Atlantic Monthly*, July 1876, pp. 93–107; "In and About the Fair," *Scribner's Monthly Magazine*, series appearing in September, October and November, 1876; and United States Centennial Commission, *International Exhibition, 1876*, U.S. Government Printing Office, Washington, 1880–1884, eleven volumes.
7. P.S. Foner, "Black participation in the Centennial of 1876," pp. 533–8.
8. William H. Crew, "Centennial Notes," Pennsylvania Magazine of History and Biography, July, 1976, quoting Diary of Henry Crew, entry for July 7, 1876.
9. *Celebration at Collinsville by the Inhabitants of The Town of Canton, Connecticut on the One Hundredth Anniversary of the Independence of the United States of America, July Fourth, 1876*, Fowler, Miller & Co., Hartford, 1877, pamphlet in the collection of the Boston Public Library; "The Centennial Celebration of American Independence at Canton, China on July Fourth, 1876," published at the office of the Daily Advertiser, Canton, 1876, pamphlet in the collection of the Boston Public Library; for examples of other celebrations, see *A Full Report of the Exercises of the Centennial Celebration of the Declaration of Independence by American Citizens in Stuttgart, Germany, July 4th, 1876*, printed by Edward Hallberger, Stuttgart, 1876, pamphlet in the collection of the John Hay Library, Brown University; *Account of the Proceedings of the Americans*

in Berlin at the Celebration of the One Hundredth Anniversary of the Declaration of Independence, July 4th, 1876, privately printed pamphlet in the collection of the Boston Public Library; *Celebration by the Inhabitants of Worcester, Mass., of the Centennial Aniversary of the Declaration of Independence, July 4, 1876*, printed by order of the City Council, Worcester, 1876; *An Account of the Celebration of the Centennial Fourth of July at Logansport, Indiana*, pamphlet in the collection of the American Antiquarian Society, Worcester, Mass.; numerous broadside Centennial programs are available in archival libraries.

10. Elizabeth Cady Stanton, Susan B. Anthony, and Mathilda Joslyn Gage, *The History of Woman Suffrage*, Volume III, Rochester, New York, 1886, p. 81.

11. Letter to James Madison, January 30, 1787, *The Writings of Thomas Jefferson*, Paul Leicester Ford, editor, G.P. Putnam's Sons, New York, 1894, Volume IV.

Glory of Empire   **10**

Vigorous celebrations marking the end of the Civil War and the national Centennial stood out against a gradual but steady decline in public Independence Day ceremonies. Celebrations that had flourished when the nation was young and uncertain about its identity seemed less necessary to a nation where industrial prosperity combined with a growing national sense of self confidence. Americans who once devoted July Fourth to the rituals of nation building now turned their attention elsewhere. Regret over the passing of Fourth of July celebrations in the traditional style sometimes inspired cities and towns to mount old-fashioned Fourth of July ceremonies, but formal exercises seemed out of date, and every year fewer committees of citizens took the trouble to organize them.

Preserving the Tradition

Henry Bowen, the wealthy New York City publisher of a popular Christian newspaper, the *Independent*, lamented the passing of traditional Fourth of July

An old-fashioned Fourth of July oration, delivered at Woodstock, Connecticut in 1870. (Harper's Weekly, July 23, 1870, p. 477)

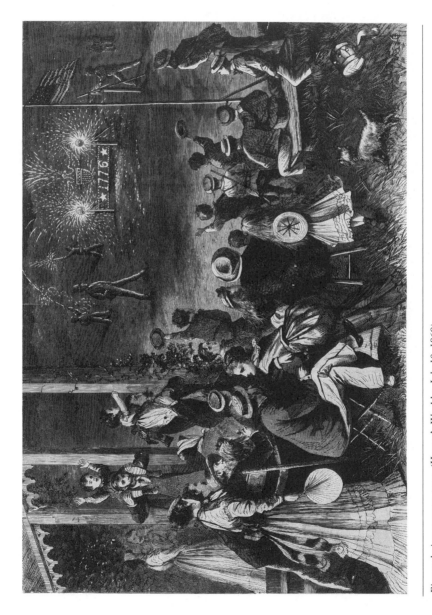

Fireworks in a country town. (Harper's Weekly, July 10, 1869)

celebrations. As a publisher, his first recourse was to use his newspaper to urge Americans to revive traditional Fourth of July exercises—but Bowen went further, staging the kind of Fourth of July celebration he thought Americans ought to have at his summer home in rural Woodstock, Connecticut. From 1870 until his death in 1896, Bowen sponsored Fourth of July exercises that drew the attention of the nation with the presence of senators, ambassadors, Cabinet members and two presidents, Ulysses S. Grant and Benjamin Harrison, who came to deliver Fourth of July orations at Woodstock during their terms of office. In 1877, Bowen opened Roseland, a privately owned, beautifully landscaped park built as a setting for his Fourth of July celebrations, but he could not stem the tide of change.[1]

Decoration Day had become the national occasion for orations and solemn civic exercises. The Fourth of July marked the beginning of summer and the migration of thousands of city dwellers to the country for the season. Decoration Day was the occasion for watching parades and feeling patriotic; the Fourth of July was the day when schools closed and amusement parks opened. Railroads, steamships and the new streetcar lines offered convenient transportation and Americans boarded them on the Fourth of July in search of a good time.

Streetcar companies frequently sought to increase summertime business by building amusement parks at the end of the line; these opened for the season on Independence Day to a flourish of trumpets and a volley of exploding fireworks. Rocky Point amusement park in Rhode Island lured patrons to its Fourth of July celebration in 1890 with a simulation of the "Bombardment of Paris" in the Franco-Prussian War. Music from several bands increased in wildness and intensity until a deafening boom of artillery was heard and fireworks exploded overhead as the band played the French rally, the German charge and the surrender—excursion tickets, 30 cents.[2]

Circuses, balloon ascensions and traveling menageries offered to entertain Fourth of July crowds, but wild West shows were favorites of the age. Buffalo Bill Cody's Wild West Show, which first opened at North Platte, Nebraska on July 4, 1883, was the best known of many wild West shows that crisscrossed the nation in special trains filled with buffalo, cow ponies and spangled costumes. Audiences in eastern cities and midwestern towns saw reenactments of such dramatic moments of real and imagined western history as "The Robbery of the Overland Mail" and "Custer's Last Rally" with a cast of "200 genuine savages, scouts, soldiers, and plainsmen."[3]

Many cities began the day by ringing bells and firing cannon, followed by lively programs of parades, band concerts, ball games, regattas, bicycle races, and evening fireworks attended mainly by those who could not spend the day in the country. Americans who could afford summer homes retreated to them on the Fourth of July, gathering family and friends for a day of picnicing and relaxation, capped by private displays of fireworks in the evening. Middle-class

Americans left their city homes on the Fourth, toting picnic suppers and boxes of fireworks to be shot off after dark. The wide variety of Fourth of July amusements and sporting events combined with the increasing rarity of long-winded orations to help the Fourth of July regain popularity in the 1880s and '90s not as a day of patriotic commemoration, but as a gay summer holiday.[4]

There were occasional serious moments on the Fourth, and, in 1881, a note of tragedy, when President Garfield was fatally wounded on July second by a gun in the hands of a disappointed office-seeker. The nation passed several mournful days, including a very subdued Fourth of July, while the president lay on his deathbed.

The historic significance of July Fourth has led generations of Americans to schedule important events on this auspicious date. In the late 19th century, politicians sought to gain stature by kicking off campaigns on the Fourth of July. Indeed, the tradition of inaugurating new enterprises on July fourth is almost as old as the republic. Earth was broken for the early canals on the Fourth of July, the great railroad bridge across the Mississippi at St. Louis was opened on July 4, 1874, by two trains, one heading east and one heading west, and in the 20th century, spaceships are launched on Independence Day.

On July 4, 1884, the government of France presented the Statue of Liberty to the United States. On July 4, 1900, Americans in Paris dedicated a monument to General Lafayette.[5] And in 1888, a great meeting of former soldiers in the Union and Confederate Armies was held on the Fourth of July on the battlefield at Gettysburg. Events in international affairs and statecraft are harder to schedule for the Fourth of July, but the trick was sometimes managed.

Politics and Imperialism

After nine years of independence, the Republic of Texas, suffering severe financial difficulties, pressed its suit for admission to the Union and Congress, which was in an expansionist mood and fearful of French and British designs on the Lone Star Republic, agreed. On July 4, 1845, Texas President Anson Jones summoned a convention to accept the terms of annexation.

American influence in the Kingdom of Hawaii increased steadily through the 19th century as sandalwood traders, missionaries, whalers and sugar planters established economic, cultural and, finally, political domination of the islands. In 1893, a group of American and Hawaiian sugar planters seeking annexation to the United States overthrew Queen Liliuokalani. President Cleveland, whose inquiries revealed that most Hawaiians opposed the coup, refused to accept annexation. On July 4, 1894, the rebel planters proclaimed the Republic of

Costumed figures riding on an elaborate horsedrawn float in the Fourth of July parade at Portland, Maine in 1886 portray a colonial town meeting. (1786-1886, Centennial Celebration of the One Hundredth Anniversary of the Incorporation of the Town of Portland. John T. Hall, editor, published by the City Council)

Costumed girls holding American flags represent each of the United States on a Victorian parade float. (1786–1886, Centennial Celebration of the One Hundredth Anniversary of the Incorporation of the Town of Portland, John T. Hall, editor, published by the City Council)

Hawaii under President Sanford Dole, who governed the islands as an independent nation until they were annexed by America during the imperial enthusiasm of the Spanish-American War.

In July 1898 the United States was engaged in a splendid little war against
Spain. At the end of the Spanish-American War, a wildly enthusisatic nation
became a global empire in possession of Cuba, Puerto Rico, Hawaii, Guam and
the Philippines. At the war's beginning, the question was how the untested
United States Navy and the tiny regular army could fight and win a war on two
oceans against the standing army and navy of an empire, even a superannuated
empire like Spain's.

Young men reared on tales of Civil War glory rushed to enlist in volunteer
regiments. The nation thrilled at news of Admiral Dewey's victory on Manila
Bay and cheered as Volunteer Colonel Teddy Roosevelt led his Rough Riders
up San Juan Hill and into fame and glory. That battle, a mismanaged, ill-planned,
minor infantry encounter, which would hardly have been noticed in a larger war,
left the Americans in possession of a hill overlooking the harbor of Santiago de
Cuba on July second. In the harbor, blockaded by American battleships, lay the
Spanish fleet under the command of Admiral Pascual Cervera y Topete. Early
on the morning of July 3, Admiral Cervera, acting under orders from his
superiors, got up steam and raced for the open sea—and the waiting American
ships.

The American fleet, whose sailors were enthusiastic but under the less than
capable command of Admiral William Sampson, was caught napping and the
Spaniards nearly escaped. Working frantically to get up steam and man their
guns, the American ships gave chase, destroying the Spanish fleet by nightfall.
Admiral Sampson's cabled account of the battle arrived in Washington at noon
on Independence Day:

> The fleet under my command offers the nation as a Fourth of July present the
> whole of Cervera's fleet.[6]

Victory over Spain ushered in a brief but intense enthusiasm for the American
empire. There were voices of responsible dissent. Many felt that the Philippines
were as entitled to self-government as the United States, but Americans on the
whole were proud to rule an empire. Possession of an empire put the United
States on a level with the great nations of Europe, encouraging the young nation
to take up the "white man's burden" and pursue mastery over the globe. For five
or six years, pride in the new imperial status dominated the national conscious-
ness.[7]

Philippine resentment of American domination was never understood by
Americans, who bestowed schools, economic development and lessons in
limited democratic self-government on dubious Filipinos. The United States
selected July 4, 1901, as the date on which the American military handed over

Citizens of Carson City, Nevada, arrive by horse and buggy for the Fourth of July parade in 1892. (Nevada State Museum)

to a civilian administration, as William Howard Taft became governor of the Phillipines. On July 4, 1946, retaining a special economic and military relationship, the United States granted independence to the Philippines.

Explosive Diversions

Prosperous and proud of their new imperial grandeur, Americans of the nineties were in a mood to celebrate the Fourth in style. A nation that had whipped the Spanish Empire and that now led the world in industrial might, invention, wealth and virtue felt that it could afford to take a day off. On Independence Day, American adults enjoyed themselves with picnics, excursions to the country, ball games and band concerts. American boys entertained themselves just as their grandfathers had—with fireworks.

With the approach of the Fourth of July, fireworks shops opened in every American city, offering prismatic whirligigs, batteries of stars, volcanos, Pharaoh's serpents eggs, yellowjackets and incendiary devices of every imaginable variety. Adults crowded these establishments as they crowd toy shops before Christmas, shopping for fiery marvels to delight the hearts of children waiting at home, or satisfying their own boyish longings. Grown men bought hundreds of dollars worth of fireworks for display at their country houses and small boys bought firecrackers by the handful. At the turn of the century, Fourth of July fireworks was a $10 million industry.[8]

Beginning days in advance and building to a crescendo on the glorious morning itself, American towns and cities resounded to the report of firecrackers, toy cannon, pistols, squibs, bombs and hand-launched fireworks of every kind. Death, maiming and the frequent fires caused by these explosives were lamented, but only an occasional voice was raised to protest the noise and destruction. One particularly charming example of these scattered protests appeared in a Christian tabloid of the era:

> The boy stood on the backyard fence,
> Whence all but him had fled;
> The flames that lit his father's barn,
> Shone just above the shed.
>
> One bunch of crackers in his hand,
> Two others in his hat,
> With piteous accents loud he cried,
> "I never thought of that!"
> A bunch of crackers to the tail
> Of one small dog he'd tied;

The dog in anguish sought the barn,
And 'mid its ruins died.

The sparks flew wide and red and hot,
They lit upon that brat;
They fired the crackers in his hand,
And eke those in his hat,

Then came a burst of rattling sound—
The boy! Where was he gone?
Ask of the winds that far around
Strewed bits of meat and bone,

And scraps of clothes and balls and tops
And nails and hooks and yarn,
The relics of the dreadful boy
That burned his father's barn."[9]

The pious editor went on to suggest that children be taught to give to the needy all of the money commonly squandered on fireworks, a suggestion not destined to meet with widespread enthusiasm. Most Americans thought boys were as entitled to set off fireworks on the Fourth of July as they were to liberty itself. The editor who dismissed complaints about noise and danger with the laconic observation, "There are worse things than fire crackers,"[10] was in better touch with the sentiments of the day than one who thought boys might be persuaded to donate to charity money they had saved to spend on firecrackers.

Early efforts to regulate the widespread and unsafe use of fireworks to celebrate the Fourth foundered on the great popularity of celebrating with flashes of gunpowder, a custom which even the reform-minded enjoyed. Julia Ward Howe participated in a successful effort to enact an ordinance banning the sale and use of all kinds of explosives in Massachusetts in the 1870s but, she recalled, "the mayor was a personal friend of our family and granted us special permission to have in our backyard our usual private celebration with firecrackers, torpedoes, rockets, etc. . . . ." The idea had apparently been to ban the dangerous fireworks in the hands of others.[11]

Early reformers were motivated by the fear that careless use of fireworks would ignite a fire that might destroy homes or entire neighborhoods. The most destructive Fourth of July fire was the great conflagration that destroyed Portland, Maine on July 4 and 5, 1866, but it was merely the largest of many. Every fire department was on the alert on Independence Day, and there were small and large fires to put out every year.

When the mayor of Cincinnati preemptorily banned the shooting of firecrackers and pistols in the streets on the Fourth of July 1875, he was

A family watches as their young son sends a fire balloon into the night sky. Fireworks lie on the ground beside a croquet mallet from the afternoon's picnic. (Harper's Weekly, *July 8, 1871, p. 671)*

American boys produce a sound and light show with bonfires, guns, firecrackers and horns. (Harper's Weekly, July 10, 1869)

condemned by responsible opinion in the city and his instructions were ignored even by the Cincinnati police who "took a general holiday and allowed the boys to have full swing."[12] The mayor of Milwaukee demonstrated a better understanding of his constituents when he met reform sentiment by declaring that he wanted 1906 "to be the noisiest Fourth Milwaukee ever had. Everybody whoop her up, and have a rousing old celebration of Independence Day. That is what it is for. I want all the boys to make all the noise they can, but to be careful of their fingers."[13]

Sentiment indulgent of the use of firecrackers on the Fourth of July was so widespread that cities with ordinances prohibiting the use of gunpowder within city limits commonly suspended them over the Fourth of July to let the boys have their fun.[14] But the wholesale firing of gunpowder in pistols, crackers and devices of every kind from anvils to rockets was too deeply rooted a custom to need the sanction of a suspended ordinance—there was not a policeman in America who would arrest a boy for lighting a firecracker on the Fourth of July.

Notes

1. The Bowen papers, including a scrapbook of Fourth of July clippings from the *Independent* and other publications, are located at the American Antiquarian Society, Worcester, Mass.
2. *Providence Daily Journal*, July 3, 1890.
3. Advertisement in *Providence Daily Journal*, July 3, 1888.
4. Period newspapers and "Memoirs of William George Bruce" (born 1856, Milwaukee), *Wisconsin Magazine of History*, September, 1933, p. 6; Marjory R. Fenerty, "West Dedham's Sock-Firing Cannon," *New England Galaxy*, Summer, 1967, p. 41; *Chronicles from the Nineteenth Century, Family Letters of Blanche Butler and Adelbert Ames*, Volume I, compiled by Blanche Butler Ames and privately issued, 1957, letters of July 4, 1873; Ralph E. Gould, *Yankee Boyhood* (Maine), Norton, N.Y., 1950, p. 189; Hugo Nisbeth, "Minnesota as Seen by Travelers, A Swedish Visitor of the Early Seventies," *Minnesota History*, Dec. 1927, pp. 402–403; "Looking Backward; Celebrating the Fourth of July," *Chicago History*, Summer 1978, pp. 120–122; *An Account of the Fourth of July, 1881 at Mason's Pond, Lake Bomoseen, Rutland County, Vermont*, Rutland County Historical Society, 1881, pamphlet in the collection of the Boston Public Library; Thomas P. Christenses, "Danish Settlement in Minnesota," *Minnesota History*, December, 1927, pp. 371–373; S. Whitney Landon, "Summers at Caspian Lake: Memories of Greensboro, Vermont, 1896–1925," *Vermont History*, Summer, 1975, pp. 197–198.

5. *Celebration of the One Hundred and Twenty Fourth Anniversary of American Independence*, printed at Paris in 1900, pamphlet in the collection of the Boston Public Lirary.

6. Walter Millis, *The Martial Spirit, A Study of Our War with Spain*, Houghton Mifflin Co., Boston, 1931, p. 314.

7. M. Wolley, "Fourth of July in Our Colonies," *Overland Monthly*, July 10, 1913, p. 71; M. Irving, "Celebrating the Fourth in Uncle Sam's New Possessions," *Woman's Home Companion*, July, 1904, pp. 24–25; "Fourth at Manila," *Nation*, September 5, 1901, p. 184; "Independence Day in Porto Rico," *Nation*, July 18, 1901, pp. 46–48.

8. *New York Times*, July 4, 1894, p. 8.

9. *Frank Leslie's Sunday Magazine*, November, 1879.

10. *Collier's*, July 4, 1903, p. 5.

11. Quoted in Lee F. Hanmer, "A Right Fourth of July," *World's Work*, May, 1911.

12. *Cleveland Leader*, July 8, 1875, p. 1.

13. Quoted in Herbert W. Horwill, "The Fourth of July in America," *Littell's Living Age*, Aug. 3, 1907, p. 305.

14. Such suspensions are commonly included in newspaper stories on holiday preparations, see for example *Cleveland Leader* of July 3, 1866, p. 4; of July 4, 1867, p. 4; of June 30, 1874, p. 4; and of July 3, 1875, p. 4.

Safe and Sane   **11**

On the morning of Independence Day, 1899, James Keeley sat at the bedside of his desperately ill daughter while the staccato percussion of exploding firecrackers shattered the quiet of the sickroom. As the little girl slept fitfully, her father was incensed by the noise in the street, which seemed to make her illness worse.

Worried though he was, James Keeley was editor of the Chicago Tribune with a daily newspaper to get out. Late in the afternoon Keeley left his daughter's bedside to telephone his secretary and was annoyed to have their conversation interrupted explosions so loud that he couldn't hear her voice. Suddenly, Keeley had an idea. During a lull in the explosions, he gave instructions to the staff: "Get reports from thirty cities on the number of killed and injured by this goddamn foolery. Let's see what it looks like."

The idea grew on him. Ten minutes after his first call Keeley was back on the line telling the staff to "make it a hundred cities.[1]

A National Problem

On July fifth, the *Tribune* ran a column of Independence Day casualties. On the sixth there were three columns. The casualty lists ran every year for the next two decades, even though readers didn't like them and the other Chicago papers opposed the practice—it was a macabre way to spoil everyone's holiday fun.

Newspapers had been publishing accounts of Fourth of July accidents since the founding of the republic, but not reports like the ones Keeley printed in the *Tribune*. The usual story describing local fires and accidental deaths caused by firing gunpowder on the Fourth ran in the back of the paper on July fifth. Brief reports detailing accidental deaths in nearby cities also appeared, but accidents will happen, and the matter-of-fact reports buried deep in the news section failed to attract much attention.

By aggregating deaths and injuries from across the nation, James Keeley took what had been perceived an an occasional unfortunate accident and made it appear as a national problem of considerable dimensions. In 1901, the *Chicago Tribune* reported 90 deaths by tetanus infections resulting from the use of fireworks and over 1,000 maimed children—missing fingers, blinded eyes and disfiguring scarring from powder burns were among the common injuries. A very few publications and citizens took notice of the *Tribune* campaign at this point, some to endorse it,[2] others to "confess to a boyish fondness for the old fashioned, reckless, noisy day."[3] More usually, Keeley's novel idea that something ought to be done to stop Fourth of July firework injuries was simply ignored.

America was entering the Progressive Era, a period when crusading reformers aimed to provide the nation with a variety of improvements ranging from sanitary meat packing to safe playgrounds for city children. The campaign for a Safe and Sane Fourth of July soon became one of the reform movements of America's Progressive Era.[4]

In 1903, the American Medical Association, headquartered in Chicago, became interested in cases of tetanus caused by fireworks. Unlike gunshot wounds, injuries caused by flying bits of exploded toy cannons and deaths in fires touched off by fireworks, death from tetanus is slow. Tetanus patients suffered a painful and lingering decline. When death came, it was often not reported as being a result of Fourth of July fireworks.

In 1903, the American Medical Association began a systematic effort to tabulate injuries and deaths caused by celebrating the Fourth of July with gunpowder.[5] Physicians reporting to the Medical Association treated 4,449 injuries, including burns, blinding, and the loss of legs, arms and hands. By requesting reports from hospitals and physicians throughout the country, and by recording Fourth of July injuries that resulted in death from lockjaw many days

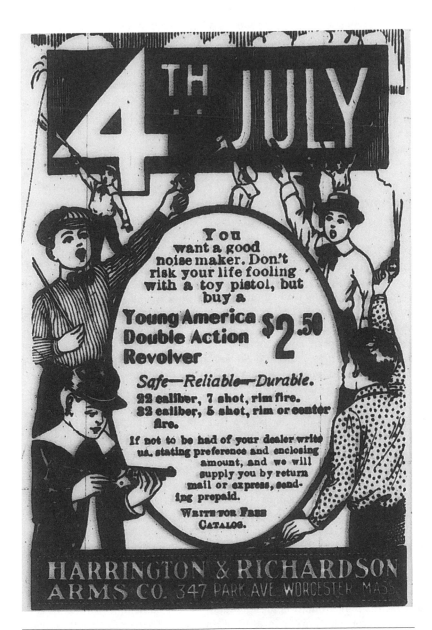

A magazine ad entices youngsters to buy fireworks and pistols. (Colliers, June 17, 1905, p. 3)

after the holiday, the Medical Association found 470 patients who had died—mostly young boys dead of lockjaw resulting from tetanus infection. This was many more casualties than the *Tribune* staff had been able to collect, and yet even this extensive list was not regarded as complete.

Aware that any criticism of traditional Fourth of July fireworks would be poorly received, the AMA took great care with the list it compiled, accurately recording the details of each case and including the type of firework responsible. Impressed by the length of its casualty list, the AMA urged legislation banning the manufacture and sale of fireworks, and a very small number of individuals began seriously to propose changes in the way the Fourth of July was celebrated.[6]

Patriotism Without Gunpowder

Professor Charles Eliott Norton of Harvard University, who spent his summers near Springfield, Massachusetts, wrote a letter to the editor of the *Springfield Republican* in 1903 suggesting that more patriotic and less dangerous ways be found to celebrate the Fourth of July. His letter inspired the formation of the Springfield Independence Day Association, one of the first groups whose purpose was "to rescue and preserve the nation's birthday from degradation and barbaric lawlessness."[7]

The Springfield Association proceeded on the wise assumption that to ban fireworks outright would be an ineffectual gesture, but children might be induced to give them up if more attractive alternatives were provided, and managed to get a modest alternative celebration off the ground. More typical was the experience of the group of reform-minded Chicagoans who incorporated an association to provide "A Sane Fourth" for the windy city, but were discouraged by the lack of support for their efforts and abandoned the attempt.[8]

In its 1903 study, the AMA found that most Fourth of July casualties resulted from superficial wounds that, in an era when tetanus vaccination was not routine, developed into lockjaw. Once this disease has developed, it is not reversible, but it is preventable by innoculating the wounded with tetanus antitoxin. Death from lockjaw as a result of minor wounds was a problem year-round, made worse on July Fourth by the frequency of injuries from toy pistols and fireworks. The American Medical Association urged doctors and hospitals to be more aggressive in innoculating even patients with minor and superficial wounds, and mounted a public-awareness campaign in June 1904 urging parents to bring children with minor wounds in for innoculation. The campaign worked. Deaths from tetanus dropped from 415 in 1903 to 91 in 1904. There were 92 non-tetanus deaths that year from cannon, gunshot and fireworks, as well as 3,986 celebration-related injuries—349 of these entailing the loss of legs, arms, hands or eyes—but the Fourth of July death toll had been reduced by more than half by the simple expedient of innoculating the wounded. By 1913 there would be only four Fourth of July deaths from tetanus.[9]

Success in reducing the death toll by better medical treatment had the paradoxical effect of prompting the AMA to redouble its efforts to outlaw fireworks. Annual editorials in its prestigious *Journal* and numerous resolutions by local medical societies urged city councils to ban the deadly fireworks. The public failed to respond to the AMA's campaign. Most parents, apparently believing that "the danger to any one child, though real, is so small as to be negligible,"[10] continued to buy fireworks for their children. Only here and there were faint stirrings of the coming impulse to take the bang out of the glorious Fourth discernable.

The editors of the *Ladies' Home Journal* entered the lists against fireworks early, sagely counseling readers that "if the boys are expected to give up fireworks, it is only fair that they should have something very good instead."[11] An appealing array of alternatives was suggested, including supervised midnight bonfires, costume parades, torchlight parades, sporting events and sunrise bell ringing—with boys allowed to pull the bell ropes.

A handful of cities moved to plan Independence Day festivities without private fireworks. Portland, Oregon was one of the first; citizen committees there sponsored a series of events to lure boys away from using fireworks in 1906. San Francisans, reeling from the terrible earthquake and fire that had destroyed the city in April, banned the sale of fireworks in July 1906. Instead, children were treated to a gala parade and an array of athletic contests.

A Modest Proposal

In the fall of 1906, Mrs. Isaac L. Rice of New York City was worried about the high level of street noise in the crowded city. Rattling trolleys, clanging fire bells, screeching brakes on elevated trains, steam whistles, boat horns and more assaulted the ears of city dwellers day and night. Mrs. Rice, who was a medical doctor, although she did not practice after her marriage, worried about the effect on health, particularly the effect on invalids and hospital patients. She founded the Society for the Supression of Unnecessary Noise to address the problem. With the approach of Independence Day 1907, Mrs. Rice issued a statement to the press requesting that revelers refrain from setting off crackers and fireworks near hospitals.[12]

It was a modest request, but a reservoir of public exasperation with the noise and hazards of celebrating Independence with exploding gunpowder had been

An Oregon family poses for the camera before enjoying their Fourth of July picnic in 1905. (Courtesy of the Oregon Historical Society, ORHI 6476)

slowly accumulating, and Mrs. Rice had inadvertantly tapped it. The response was so enthusiastic that Mrs. Rice warmed to her subject.

Four days after requesting that boys set off their caps at a courteous distance from hospitals, she was condemning the use of fireworks categorically on the grounds that "this day of days is too beautiful . . . to be desecrated with senseless racket," and charging that those who set off fireworks are "absolutely ignorant of what our glorious day stands for."[13]

Fireworks sales for 1907 were not diminished in the least by Mrs. Rice's pronouncements, but with the publication of an article entitled "Our Barbarous Fourth," in the June 1908 issue of *Century Magazine*, she became the leading voice of the movement to ban fireworks.

National Reform

In 1908, anti-fireworks sentiment, which had been building for several years,[14] jelled into a national campaign for a Safe and Sane Fourth. Straightforward concern with Fourth of July injuries and fatalities, which prompted the concern of the American Medical Association, and adult annoyance with noise, which aroused Editor Keeley and Mrs. Rice, explain only part of the impulse to reform the Fourth. As was the case with many Progressive reforms, the movement for a Safe and Sane Fourth was prompted, in part, by a concern with the changes that mass immigration had wrought in American society.

When the Independence Day Association of Springfield, Massachusetts lamented the "barbaric lawlessness which had come with our increasing population to characterize" observance of the Fourth, the implication was that the increasing population came from parts of Europe where the people were barbaric.[15] Infusing the Fourth of July with lessons in American history and patriotism would "open the hearts of . . . the alien within our gates to at least a partial significance of what to honor in our national festival."[16]

Reform committees condescendingly sought to Americanize the immigrants and instruct them in patriotism by inviting immigrant groups to march as units in Fourth of July parades. Members of one typical Independence Day committee did not expect much of these immigrant marching units, until the Polish group showed up for the parade with "uniforms, and a band, and appeared, to everyone's surprise, in military order." In fact, the Polish unit marched and wheeled with such splendid precision that they drew first prize from a parade committee left wondering how a group of factory hands reputedly prone to drunken brawling could march so handsomely.[17]

It is odd that progressive opinion turned against fireworks several years after the number of Fourth of July fatalities had been permanently reduced by stepped-up administration of tetanus antitoxin. Some of the impetus for the campaign for Safe and Sane Fourths of July resulted from a simple concern for safety, but many of the reformers had a more complex agenda in mind. Middle-class Americans felt their national identity threatened by immigrants from different cultural traditions. They desired to strengthen American cultural identity by reemphasizing the historical traditions associated with Independence Day, and the movement to ban fireworks was, to a degree, a pretext for replacing them with something more patriotic. It would have been hard for a reformer working to ban fireworks to make an appeal beginning, "The number of deaths from fireworks has declined in recent years . . ." so statistics were quoted in a more helpful manner. Reformers repeatedly cited aggregate casualty figures instead of separating figures for serious injuries from those for minor wounds.

The *Journal of the American Medical Association* continued to publish careful tables of Fourth of July deaths and injuries, but in 1908 the "grand totals" at the bottom of the table were cumulative figures from the period 1903–1908. An interested reader had carefully to trace columns of fine print to discover the figures for 1908 alone.

Lee Hanmer, associate director of the Department of Child Hygiene of the progressive Russell Sage Foundation, which took an active role in the Safe and Sane Fourth campaign, cited figures showing that the average number killed and injured each year from 1903 to 1910 in America's 83 largest cities was 4,543. This gave the misleading appearance of a steady number of casualties, at a time when they were actually declining.

Mrs. Rice blithely printed statistics comparing Fourth of July casualties to those of seven famous Revolutionary War battles. This remarkable statistical table compares the 449 "killed and wounded" at the Battle of Bunker Hill with the 4,169 "killed and wounded" on July 4, 1904, the 37 "killed and wounded," at Ft. Moultrie, with the 5,176 "killed and wounded" on July 4, 1905, and so forth.[18] It was a cleverly misleading way of exaggerating the seriousness of injuries from Fourth of July fireworks. The 163 deaths and 345 serious injuries in 1908 were bad enough, but progressive magazines and newspaper editorials reported only the appaling news that 5,623 Americans had been killed or wounded by Independence Day celebrations.[19]

The campaign worked. In 1909 and 1910, cities across the nation instituted "Safe and Sane" celebrations of Independence Day. Programs were planned and implemented by local citizens' committees, inspired by national progressive magazines and institutions.[20] The Municipal Conference of the Playground Congress, a national progressive organization that gathered for its annual meeting at Pittsburgh from May 10 to 14, 1909, heard a series of speakers on the topic of a sane and safe Fourth of July. The Congress endorsed reform measures and offered advice to its members on banning fireworks and instituting

"TO THE FOURTH!"

Figures representing Death and the "Fireworks Trust" toast the Fourth of July with champagne in this Progressive Era political cartoon. (From Life Magazine, June 29, 1911)

Floats in the 1910 Fourth of July parade at Buffalo, New York portray "The Old Fourth," with children wrapped in bandages, and "The New Fourth." (The World's Work, May 1911)

such alternative activities as band concerts, public firework displays and field day events.[21]

The Russell Sage Foundation printed and distributed brochures describing alternative Fourth of July celebrations and even produced a movie as part of its anti-fireworks campaign. In this quintessential melodrama the mayor, a handsome widower with a young son, turns a deaf ear to the appeals of a "Sane Fourth" committee headed by a pretty widow with a young daughter, listening instead to villainous fireworks dealers who urge a traditionally noisy Fourth. When the mayor's son is injured by fireworks, blindness and lockjaw threaten. The pretty widow nurses the mayor's son back to health; the mayor falls in love with her and signs a "Sane Fourth" ordinance for the coming year.[22]

A New Style of Celebration

Fourth of July reformers were sincerely concerned about the large number of Fourth of July deaths and injuries, but it was also true that high casualty figures won public support for reforming the Fourth in ways that would suit both the reformers' tastes and their goals of instilling patriotism in American children and American attitudes in immigrants. The tastes of progressive reformers ran toward patriotic pageants, patriotic music, parades with patriotic floats, marching units patriotically costumed in period dress, and tableaux vivants depicting patriotic scenes in American history. They also favored English folk dancing. Reels and Morgan dances were a kind of upper-class fad in the early years of the century, as Americans of Anglo-American descent drew on their own ethnic heritage in an effort to reassert cultural hegemony in the face of large-scale immigration.

Taste aside, the pressing need was for programs appealing enough to entice lower-class men and children in general to give up firecrackers and attend the planned festivities. Banning firecrackers alone wouldn't work, since without alternative activities fireworks were too appealing, but innovative enforcement was tried. Police in Council Bluffs, Iowa deputized 10-year-olds and sent them out to round up their miscreant buddies. One little fellow dragged another boy in by the collar instructing the police to "book him" as a "repeat offender." When asked how he could know that, the cheeky deputy replied that he knew for sure because the two had set off firecrackers together early that very morning.[23]

Springfield, Massachusetts, which was first in the field, became a national model of a successful Safe and Sane Fourth of July. Independence Day 1910 in Springfield began at 6 A.M. with the pealing of bells. From nine until eleven o'clock, a Military and Historical Parade passed through town. There were adults and children costumed to represent marching units of Indians, Puritans,

Proponents of a Sane Fourth confront the Mayor in a scene from the Russell Sage Foundation propaganda movie, A Sane Fourth of July. *(Advertising pamphlet for* A Sane Fourth of July, *W.C. Langdon papers, Brown University Library)*

Later scene at the bedside of the Mayor's son as he suffers from fireworks-induced injuries. (Advertising pamphlet for A Sane Fourth of July, *W.C. Langdon papers, Brown University Library)*

Minute Men, Continentals, British Regulars, Hessians, sailors and cowboys. The parade boasted a unit of Spanish-American War veterans, but the highlight was the appearance of 200 veterans of the Civil War. A group of Confederate veterans from Petersburg, Virginia traveled to Springfield and marched in a gesture of reconciliation; members of the Grand Army of the Republic marched alongside their erstwhile foes and even had a veteran's marching band.

Forty-five years after the war ended, the South was not yet fully reintegrated into national life. Southern states did not participate in the campaign for a Safe and Sane Fourth; the holiday had not fully regained its antebellum popularity in Dixie, and Fourth of July tetanus and firework injuries were consequently not a large problem. Southern physicians worried about tetanus at Christmastime, for that was when southerners were likely to fire off celebratory rounds of gunpowder. Only after the Second World War would the South again celebrate the Fourth of July as fully as the rest of the Union.

In 1910, Springfield was excited by the presence of veterans of both the blue and gray armies, but the Independence Day Association was proudest of the presence of representatives of so many ethnic groups in the National Historical Section of the parade. There were floats and costumed marchers representing the culture and achievements of Assyria, Babylonia, Persia, Egypt, Greece, Rome, Israel, France, Germany, Scotland, Sweden and Poland.[24]

At eleven o'clock, Springfield enjoyed a band concert of patriotic music, followed at noon by a national salute of 46 guns—the Association was not opposed to all noise, only unscheduled noise. The afternoon was filled with field day events, sporting events and band concerts in the city parks. At night, the citizens of Springfield could gather to watch an illuminated boat parade at the riverfront, or admire public fireworks displays offered at four locations. Parades, pageants, concerts of patriotic music, field day events and public fireworks were the mainstays of reformed Fourth of July celebrations throughout the nation.[25]

Many communities mounted ambitious costume pageants in honor of Independence Day. Some reenacted a dramatic moment of local history, such as an Indian raid. Others chose important events in the building of American nationhood; the life of Washington was a favorite, outdone in popularity only by plays depicting the Contintental Congress debating and voting for Independence. Most common were mixed pageants with lots of costumes and lots of parts, like the Fourth of July pageant produced at the University of Illinois in 1918.

It began with patriotic recitations by characters dressed to represent "Illinois" and "America." They were followed by "Thomas Jefferson" and "members" of the Continental Congress reading excerpts from the Declaration of Independence. After the audience joined in singing the "Star Spangled Banner," "General Washington" read from the Constitution. Then came an oration and several songs, including "On Forever, Illinois." Since the United States had just entered a popular war, the heart of the pageant depicted "America" joining

A small-town Fourth of July parade marches up the main street of Langlois, Oregon in 1915. (Courtesy of the Oregon Historical Society, ORHI 35674)

THE FOURTH OF JULY IS COMING

Is your city ready with a fireworks ordinance under which sanity can be patriotic?

THE OLD WAY
An annual orgy of noise and death and fire

Drawings prepared for THE AMERICAN CITY *by* MORRIS

THE NEW WAY
Public celebrations in parks and open spaces under municipal supervision

Editorial cartoon depicts the dangers of the old-style Fourth and the joys of the new. (American City, May 1927, p. 605)

This Viking ship represents ethnic participation in a Safe and Sane Fourth of July parade. (Advertising pamphlet for A Sane Fourth of July, *W.C. Langdon papers, Brown University Library)*

characters representing Belgium, France, Britain and Italy as she calls her sons to join European "Soldiers of the Great War" fighting for democracy.[26]

Reformers promoting Safe and Sane Fourths of July achieved a fair measure of success.[27] Many municipal and state authorities banned or restricted fireworks, and even where they remained legal, some of the worst types were eliminated. The toy pistols firing blank cartriges that caused so much tetanus and the giant firecrackers that blew off so many childish fingers were effectively eliminated in favor of less lethal types that became known, paradoxically, as "safe and sane fireworks." In consequence of the new restrictions on firework sales, Fourth of July deaths and injuries were dramatically reduced. By 1913 there were only 32 deaths and 1,163 injuries from fireworks nationwide.[28]

Even the goal of including immigrants in the festivities was largely fulfilled, although this was not entirely the result of progressive efforts. The truth was that immigrant communities loved America, were eager for Americanization and participated gladly in the parades and flag waving. One immigrant group went even further, becoming so thoroughly Americanized that they decided to export the Fourth of July back to the old country.

In 1911, the Danish American Association purchased several hundred acres of Danish moorland for presentation to their mother country as a park. The Rebild National Park contains an Emigrant Archives Building, an emigration museum with a log cabin, and, once a year, a transplanted Fourth of July celebration complete with picnics and orations.[29]

The patriotic pageants, parades, thousands of American flags given to schoolchildren and band concerts of American music reinstilled the patriotic theme of Independence Day. Whereas the late 19th-century Fourth had been a summer holiday punctuated by the incessant noise of exploding gunpowder, the Safe and Sane style Fourth was a recognizably patriotic celebration.

Notes

1. John Tebbel, *An American Dynasty; The Story of the McCormicks, Medills and Pattersons*, 1947, Doubleday & Co., Garden City, N.Y., pp. 78–79.
2. *The Independent*, July 17, 1902, pp. 1737–1738.
3. *The Atlantic Monthly*, "On Keeping the Fourth of July," July, 1902, p. 3; *Collier's*, July 4, 1902, July 2, 1904.

4. William H. Cohn, "Popular Culture and Social History," *Journal of Popular Culture*, summer, 1977, p. 167–179.

5. *Journal of the American Medical Association*, August 19, 1903, pp. 547–559.

6. "Prevention of Our Annual Holocaust," *The Independent*, November 26, 1903, pp. 2821–2822; *Collier's*, July 3, 1906.

7. *Official Program of the Independence Day Association of Springfield, Massachusetts*, 1910, pamphlet in the William C. Langdon collection, John Hay Library, Brown University.

8. "Fourth of July Tetanus," *Journal of the American Medical Association*, September 3, 1904, p. 668.

9. "Fourth of July Tetanus," *Journal of the American Medical Association*, Sept. 3, 1904, p. 670; and "Eleventh Annual Summary of Fourth of July Injuries," August 30, 1913, p. 679.

10. *New York Times*, editorial, July 7, 1905, p. 6.

11. "A Fourth of July Without Fireworks, Some Sane and Safe Ways to Celebrate the Great American Holiday," *Ladies Home Journal*, June, 1907, p. 42.

12. *New York Times*, June 30, 1907, part 2, p. 7.

13. *New York Times*, July 3, 1907, p. 5.

14. "Accidents on the Fourth," *Outlook*, June 22, 1907, pp. 354–355; "Hazards of the Fourth of July," *Independent*, June 20, 1907, p. 1485; "Must the Slaughter Go On?," *Outlook*, June 6, 1908, p. 280; "Let the Children be Killed," *Ladies Home Journal*, July, 1908, p. 3; and numerous newspaper editorials.

15. *Official Program of the Independence Day Association of Springfield, Massachusetts, 1910*, pamphlet in the William C. Langdon collection, John Hay Library, Brown University.

16. Mrs. Isaac L. Rice, "Our Barbarous Fourth," *Century Magazine*, June 1908.

17. "How One Town Spends the Fourth," *Ladies Home Journal*, June, 1908, p. 47.

18. Lee F. Hanmer, "A Right Fourth of July," *World's Work*, May, 1911; Mrs. Isaac L. Rice, "For a Safe and Sane Fourth," *The Forum*, March 1910, p. 233.

19. For example, "The Toll of the Fourth; 'Harmless' Devices resulting in 29,296 Killed and Wounded in the Past Six Years," *Collier's*, July 2, 1910, p. 15.

20. "New Fourth of July," *Independent*, July 1, 1909, pp. 44–45; "Reforming the Fourth," *The Nation*, July 15, 1909, pp. 47–48; Bouck White, "What the Neighbors Did," *Country Life in America*, July 1913, pp. 59–60; Mrs. Isaac L. Rice, "For a Safe and Sane Fourth," *The Forum*, March, 1910, pp. 217–237; Lee F. Hamner, "A Right Fourth of July; How to Prepare for a Jubilant Holiday," *The World's Work*, May, 1911; "Daniel Boone, Patriot, A Fourth of July Pageant for Boys," and "The Boston Tea-Party, A One Act Play for Young People," *The Delineator*, July, 1911.

21. *How a City Can Celebrate Independence Day Without Loss of Life or Fire Damage*; also see *A Safe and Patriotic Fourth of July*, published by the Committee on Independence Day Celebrations of the Art Department, New Jersey State Federation of Women's Clubs, pamphlets in the William C. Langdon Collection, John Hay Library, Brown University.

22. The Russell Sage Foundation has no copy of the movie. A pamphlet describing it is entitled, *The Story of a Moving Picture Film Entitled 'A Sane Fourth of July'*; this and other Russell Sage pamphlets including, *The More Patriotic Fourth*; *Cities Having a Sane Celebration, July 4th, 1910*; *Printed Matter Distributed, Fourth of July Campaign, 1910*; *Independence Day Celebrations*; *A Safer, Saner Fourth of July With More Patriotism and Less Noise*; *Independence Day Legislation and Celebration Suggestions*; *Suggestions for Celebrating Independence Day*; and *Suggestions for the Celebration of the Fourth of July by Means of Pageantry*, by William Chauncy Langdon, 1912, are available in the William C. Langdon Collection, John Hay Library, Brown University.

23. *New York Times*, July 1, 1907, p. 16.

24. *The Springfield Daily Republican*, July 5, 1910, pp. 8–10.

25. Henry Litchfield West, "A Safe and Sane Fourth of July," *The Forum*, August, 1909, pp. 105–112; J. E. Cutler, "Cleveland's New Fourth of July," *The Survey*, June, 1910, pp. 507–510; "'Sane' Fourth for New York," *The Survey*, May 7, 1910, pp. 194–5; "How One Town Celebrates the Glorious Fourth," *Country Life in America*, July, 1916.

26. "Fourth of July Pageant for the University of Illinois, 1918," William C. Langdon Collection, Brown University.

27. P. Mackaye, "The New Fourth of July," *Century*, July, 1910, p. 394–6; "Figures Show a Safer, Saner Fourth," *American City*, October, 1916, pp. 428–9; "Fourth Sane and Nearly Safe," *Literary Digest*, July 17, 1915, p. 182; "The Growing Sanity of Fourth of July Celebrations," *American City*, June 1913, pp. 654–655.

28. "Eleventh Annual Summary of Fourth of July Injuries," *Journal of the American Medical Association*, Aug. 30, 1913, pp. 679–685.

29. Agnes Rothery, *Denmark, Kingdom of Reason*, Viking Press, New York, 1937, pp. 96–99.

Backyard Holiday 12

In 1917 the United States mobilized to repay a debt to our oldest ally. France and Britain had been fighting German aggression for three weary years, but lacked the resources to achieve a military victory. Germany, equally drained of resources, refused to end the war by negotiation.

While President Wilson spent the winter of 1916–1917 in futile efforts to make peace, Germany pushed to win the war and expand its territory. The German government attempted to keep the Americans occupied on this side of the Atlantic by scheming to induce Mexico to attack the American Southwest, and responded to mediation proposals by demanding the annexation of Luxembourg, a strip of eastern France, and the Russian Baltic provinces, along with protectorates over Belgium and Poland.

There were some Americans who wanted to enter the war allied with Germany, and many, President Wilson foremost among them, who sincerely wanted peace. But France was our oldest ally; England was our mother country; and Germany was the aggressor. Throughout 1915 and 1916, an increasing stream of supplies reached France and Great Britain on American shipping. Germany's attempt to cut the allied nations off from America by authorizing unrestricted U-boat attacks on American shipping was the provocation that finally brought America into the World War I. On April 2, 1917, President Wilson appeared before Congress to urge American entry into a war to make the world "safe for democracy."

Wartime Celebrations

America, with a small standing army, few battleships, virtually no military airplanes or tanks, and very few munitions factories, was almost wholly unprepared for war. President Wilson gave command of the American Expeditionary Force to General John J. Pershing, who had been a lieutenant at San Juan Hill, and sent him to France to wait for an army to be recruited and trained. At the end of June the first American fighting units landed at St.-Nazaire on the French coast. The three battalions that had arrived were far too few to affect the course of war, nothing at all compared to the 2 million doughboys who would be in Europe by the war's end. But an exhausted French nation welcomed them with delirious joy: they represented the hope of victory.

Responding to the French need for symbolic encouragement, since the material assistance of a substantial American fighting force could not arrive for weeks or months, the men of the 16th Infantry were rushed from the coast to Paris to participate in Fourth of July celebrations.

Cheering crowds thronged the streets as a city that had abandoned hope of victory saw its saviors arrive. Americans were festooned with wreaths and ropes of flowers, leading General Pershing to remark that his men looked like "a moving flower garden." The parade halted at Pipcus cemetery and the grave of Lafayette. Speaker after speaker addressed the jubilant crowd in a volley of Fourth of July oratory praising French heroism and the Franco-American alliance, but the words of one man are remembered. General Pershing had delegated his oratorical obligation to Colonel C. E. Stanton, who rose to pledge American dedication to the alliance and closed with a simple statement of American sentiment that reverberated in the hearts of two nations, "Lafayette, we are here."[1]

America was only in the war for a year and a half, but the Fourth of July 1918 was celebrated with all of the enthusiasm that fighting a popular war lends to patriotic festivals. Doughboys and proudly uniformed Navy "yeomanettes," America's first enlisted women, paraded up avenues bedecked with the red, white and blue flags of America, England and France, while wartime Fourth of July pageants depicted scenes from the French Revolution and the signing of the Magna Carta. Patriotic tableaux vivants featured characters representing Belgian suffering, German autocracy, and American liberty.[2] Tens of thousands of American boys spent Independence Day in the trenches, comforted only by the certainty that they were fighting for freedom. Back from the front lines, American soldiers in Italy, France and England celebrated the Fourth by listening to orations, holding Fourth of July dinners and playing baseball. In London, George V (great-great-grandson of the king whom Thomas Jefferson branded a tyrant in his immortal Declaration) attended a baseball game—the United States Army played the United States Navy.[3]

America marked victory on the Fourth of July 1919 with the greatest parade ever to march down New York's Fifth Avenue,[4] but postwar Fourth of July celebrations revealed the familiar pattern of a fading reform impulse. During the crusade to make the Fourth of July safe and sane, volunteers stepped forward to stitch dozens of costumes, hammer together elaborate floats and organize hundreds of youngsters for dancing, marching and field day events. The enthusiasm of the organizers combined with anti-firework statutes to reduce the use of fireworks for a few years; then the enthusiasm wore off.

Parades, orations, pageants, sporting and field day events, even formal exercises, continued to be staged on a more or less elaborate scale by communities able to muster a committee willing to do the work, but as America prospered and concern over the cultural threat posed by immigration abated, fewer volunteers appeared and fewer community celebrations were planned. Not even the increasing efforts of the new municipal recreation departments could make up for the dearth of volunteers. Amusements and private parties supplanted the patriotic parades and pageants of the Progressive Era, and Fourth of July in the 1920s again belonged to boys and firecrackers. Some of the most dangerous sorts, notably six-inch firecrackers and large blank cartridges for flimsy toy pistols, had been partially eliminated by firework control statutes, but rockets, cherry bombs, Roman candles and smaller firecrackers were much in evidence.

Fourth of July celebrations were dampened by the hardships of the Great Depression, which reduced the budgets of municipal recreation departments and left little spare money for Americans to spend on bunting, costumes and elaborate parades. Such traditional celebrations as the annual small-town baseball game between married and single men went on despite the hard times, joined by celebrations arising from the superheated political atmosphere of the era. In 1937, New Yorkers could watch the elderly United American Spanish War Veterans raise the flag at City Hall Park or participate in the annual celebration of the Tammany Society, always lively in an election year, but they could also attend Fourth of July celebrations sponsored by the Communist Party of New York and the Italian Anti-Fascist Committee.[5]

In Europe that year, American volunteers fighting fascism in Spain with the American Lincoln and George Washington Battalions celebrated the Fourth of July outside Madrid, with fireworks provided by artillery engagements not far from the city. War, which had already broken out in Spain, Ethiopia and China, would soon envelop the world, but in the late nineteen thirties, Americans read the frightening headlines of a world at war in a nation still at peace. As late as July Fourth 1941, Emperor Hirohito politely cabled Independence Day greetings to President Roosevelt.[6] Five months later, his air force bombed Pearl Harbor and our nation was at war.

Faced with the spectre of brutal Japanese conquest of Asia and the Nazi drive to rule the entire western world, the United States focused its energies on fighting and winning the largest war in its history. Never before, not even during the Civil War, had the nation devoted its resources so completely to a war effort, and many holiday traditions were pushed aside to make sure that the effort succeeded. Few Fourth of July celebrations were held during the war, but at military bases, this day was chosen for ceremonies at which medals were presented to the parents and widows of men killed in action.

The traditional family automobile excursion was out. Everyone recognized the need to conserve gasoline for use in tanks and airplanes, and anyone who wasted precious fuel on so frivolous an expedition as a picnic was likely to be picked up by officials of the Office of Price Administration. Tremendous crowds thronged railroad and airline terminals, trying for the few available seats, but most Americans spent the day quietly at home.

In 1943, the Fourth of July fell on a Sunday. Always before, this had meant a postponed celebration and a Monday holiday, but the tradition of moving Independence Day to Monday out of respect for the Sabbath was swept aside by the pressing need to maintain wartime production. After a quiet Sunday, factories opened on Monday morning and the war effort went forward. When the war was over, Americans came to think of a Fourth of July that fell on Sunday as a three-day weekend, but few actual celebratory exercises were postponed from Sunday to Monday in deference to the Sabbath.

Americans did without many commodities urgently needed by the armed forces. There were no silk stockings, silk was needed for parachutes; there was no rubber, it was made into tires for military vehicles; and there were no fireworks, since the entire capacity of the explosives and gunpowder industries was devoted to wartime production. What the efforts of concerned parents, progressive reformers and municipal authorities had failed to accomplish, was summarily effected by the war. On the Fourth of July, for the first time in American history, everything was quiet. But in 1944, American troops in Europe made up for the silence of their younger brothers and sisters at home by celebrating the Fourth of July with a bang.

A month after D-Day, allied troops were fighting hard along a hundred-mile front, trying to break out of the Normandy beachhead. The United States Army always honors Independence Day with a national salute, one salvo for every state. On July Fourth, 1944, the Army outdid itself. General Omar Bradley arranged to have every artillery piece on the front fixed on a target and fired at the precise moment of noon on the Fourth of July. At that instant, a clap of thunder exploded across the French countryside as 1,100 shells burst on German targets in a glorious national salute to freedom.[7]

Independence Day Loses Its Bang

Intense concern about the dangers of fireworks, which had characterized Progressive Era holiday preparations, had been renewed in 1937 when the National Fire Protection Association published a model statute designed to ban the sale and use of fireworks. Four states enacted fireworks bans in 1939 in a campaign that was renewed after the war when state after state enacted fireworks ban or control statutes. By 1953, 28 of the 48 states banned all private fireworks, and 14 other states and the District of Columbia restricted sales to specified, smaller varieties.[8]

There were (and are) no safe fireworks. Every year, children receive eye injuries and serious burns from "harmless" sparklers. Bottle-rockets and Roman candles, regarded as "safe" fireworks and therefore legal in many states, cause severe injuries, particularly eye injuries, but also serious burns and the loss of fingers. Among the thousands of annual injuries are a small but tragic number of debilitating burns, missing limbs, blindings and deaths.

Anti-fireworks campaigns took the bang out of the Fourth of July. And if the holiday became much safer, it was also far more dull than the boisterous day familiar to earlier generations of Americans. The continual percussion of exploding caps, the aroma of gunsmoke and the backyard glory of fireworks bursting in the darkness defined Independence Day and set it apart. Once private fireworks were reduced to a faint echo of their former ear-splitting, eye-catching domination, a note of nostalgia was heard for the old holiday, noisy and dangerous—but fun![9] Like much else in the sober 1950s, the glorious Fourth of July was boring.

Postwar America, as proud and patriotic as before, was uncertain how to spend the Fourth of July until the municipal fireworks began at nightfall. Community pageants and parades had marched into history and hardly anyone thought of giving a Fourth of July oration. The Fourth became a day of a thousand programs, and none at all. There were beauty contests and auto races, rodeos and regattas from coast to coast. Some towns had parades, some had concerts, a few even had formal exercises with orations, but there was no public event unique to the Fourth of July. Independence Day is a summer holiday and, usually, a long weekend, making it a wonderful time to schedule everything from dog shows to parachute-jumping contests. The daytime hours offered no modern equivalent of the costume pageants and field day events of the turn of the century, the parades of the Victorian era, and the formal exercises, orations and dinners of the early republic, because the most prosperous and supremely self-assured generation in American history felt no need to affirm its national identity. America was the mightiest, wealthiest and best nation the world had ever seen. What could a speech or a pageant add?

With help from Uncle Sam in the form of GI mortgages, the generation that fought and won the war moved into new suburban communities springing up across the landscape. Postwar prosperity enabled tens of thousands of Americans to acquire station wagons, backyards and a passion for the backyard barbecue. The mouth-watering aroma of hamburgers sizzling on a charcoal grill became the quintessential scent of Independence Day, as a new tradition, the backyard Fourth of July barbecue, was born.

Friends and family gathered, bringing salads and watermelon. A volleyball net was streched between two trees; a game of baseball started on the lawn. The summer day was long, lazy and informal, with lots of time to talk, drink beer and pitch a few horseshoes before sunset, when everyone drove to the beach or the high school field to watch the town fireworks display.

The backyard Fourth of July of the 1950s and '60s was a party without fireworks. Fireworks were illegal in the larger cities and in most states and, although there was a brisk trade in illegal fireworks, these were things of the wicked city. Many children grew to adulthood in the suburbs without ever setting off a firecracker. Then, in the 1970s, the decades-long trend toward stricter controls on the sale and use of fireworks began to turn around.

"Safe" Fireworks

In 1973 the Consumer Product Safety Commission, recounting grisly stories of Fourth of July fireworks injuries, began to consider a ban on all fireworks, even the small, "safe" kind.[10] According to the Commission, small bottle rockets are unstable and often go off sideways, causing serious injury, while small firecrackers tempt small children to combine the powder for larger effect, with disastrous results. The Commission cited a horrifying catalog of injuries.

In the spring of 1974, the Consumer Product Safety Commission announced its decision to ban all firecrackers and most fireworks, and the fireworks industry blew up. A frantic lobbying campaign was mounted to induce the Commission to reverse a decision that threatened a multi-million dollar industry.

A fireworks ban was in step with the increased attention to product safety that marked the 1970s, but fatally out of step with the pro-business attitudes of the Nixon administration. Fireworks were patently unsafe even when properly used, and they invited improper and dangerous use. Manufacturers, claiming

A backyard Fourth of July barbecue at the home of the author's family in Old Saybrook, Connecticut in 1954. (Personal collection of the author)

that they would lose $50 million in 1974 sales if firecrackers were banned, fought hard to keep a portion of their products legal. They were working to protect an even larger annual profit from the sale of illegal fireworks, ostensibly manufactured or imported for sale in states where fireworks are legal, but resold at high mark-ups in states where fireworks are banned. And the fireworks industry feared that bans on bottle rockets and Roman candles would follow the ban on firecrackers.

The Consumer Product Safety Commission backed down, proscribing only the large crackers that were already outlawed by 32 states. With bureaucratic legerdemain, this victory for the fireworks industry was announced as a ban on dangerous firecrackers that would protect consumers. The final CPSC ruling, announced just in time for the Bicentennial, defined one-inch firecrackers containing no more than 50 milligrams of explosive as safe, along with small rockets, Roman candles, fountains, and party poppers.[11] Federal definition of these items as safe initiated a wave of repeals of state firework ordinances.

Americans love to set off fireworks on the Fourth of July. It took half a century of persistant campaigning to persuade most of the nation that fireworks were so dangerous that they ought to be banned; when the Consumer Product Safety Commission officially certified small fireworks as safe, it took less than a decade to persuade more than half of the state legislatures that had banned fireworks to legalize them again. Legislators could please a wealthy lobbying group by voting for a bill that would make many constituents happy. By 1988, it was legal to set off fireworks in 32 states, and eager celebrants in many states where fireworks were illegal could drive across the state line and bring home a box full of excitement.[12] Backyard barbecues of the 1980s are accompanied by the whizz-pop of rockets bursting in air.

Independence Day De-Politicized

The backyard Fourth of July is a supremely private tradition, a gathering of selected friends held in a private place with the simple intention of passing a pleasant afternoon. It is a marked change from the inclination of earlier generations to enjoy a holiday by gathering as a community in a public place. And it is a dramatic departure from traditional uses of the Fourth of July to solidify national identity, improve the moral tone of the community or forward some political cause.

Only occasionally have politics intruded on the Fourth of July in this century, and in every case the intrusion has been made by people who felt that their American identity was threatened.

In the early years of this century, many Americans felt their cultural identity threatened by large-scale immigration of people who spoke different languages, practiced different customs and were steeped in the traditions of a foreign culture. The Progressive campaigns to Americanize immigrants by introducing historical and patriotic pageantry on the Fourth of July were one response to the cultural threat posed by immigration. The effort to proclaim the Fourth of July "Americanization Day" was another.

Americanization Day was an early 20th-century effort to promote the Fourth of July as the day on which citizens would be naturalized across the nation.[13] Several cities held large naturalization ceremonies on July 4, 1915, and the idea has been used sporadically ever since, although never with the uniformity desired by its Progressive promoters.

A very different response to the perceived cultural threat posed by immigration and by Americans of different color or religion was given by members of the Ku Klux Klan. In the 1920s, members of this white, Protestant, supremicist organization sometimes chose to hold marches and rallys on the Fourth of July as a way of asserting that they, and not those whom they feared, were the "real" Americans.[14]

In the 1960s and '70s, conservative Americans felt threatened by their own children. Tension created by massive social change and counterculture assaults on the accepted mores of middle-class life, made many Americans angry and resentful. Richard Nixon, elected president by this "silent majority," urged his constituency in pre-Fourth of July exhortations to stand up and say "what's right with America." And they did.

On July 4, 1970, the "silent majority" turned out for a massive Honor America Day celebration in Washington, D. C. Reverend Billy Graham, the politically conservative evangelical minister, organized the event, which featured preaching, singing and a giant flag on the steps of the Lincoln Memorial. Police lines were set up to separate the silent majority from members of the counterculture they so feared, who had come to mock their strait-laced patriotism with a marijuana "smoke-in" and a Reflecting Pool "wade-in."

In this mood of unsettlingly rapid changes and deep social divisions, America prepared to celebrate its bicentennial.

Notes

1.   Frank E. Vandiver, *Black Jack; The Life and Times of John J. Pershing*, Texas A & M University Press, College Station, 1977, p. 724; *New York Times*, July 5, 1917, p. 1.

2. "Fighting for Freedom," July 4, 5, 6, 7, 1918, Municipal Theater, Forest Park, St. Louis, brochure in the collection of the Boston Public Library; and newspaper accounts.

3. "A Declaration of Interdependence; Commemoration in London in 1918 of the Fourth of July, 1776," published by the Library of War Literature, New York; "Festa Nazionale Americana; Roma IV Luglio, MCMXVIII," printed by Beatitti & Tumminelli, Milano, both pamphlets in the collection of the Boston Athenaeum; "A Fourth of July at the Front," *Wisconsin Magazine of History*, March 1919.

4. *New York Times*, July 4, 1918, p. 1.

5. New York Times, July 4, 1937, p. 1.

6. New York Times, July 5, 1937; July 5, 1941, p.1.

7. Omar N. Bradley, *A Soldier's Story*, 1951, Henry Holt and Co., New York, pp. 324–325.

8. *Literary Digest*, July 23, 1927, p. 12, July 18, 1931, p. 7, and July 26, 1937, p. 4; *The Playground*, July, 1926, p. 229; *Life Magazine*, July 4, 1955, p. 53; *New York Times*, July 3, 1961, p. 17.

9. G. B. Wesson, *The American Mercury*, July 1960, pp. 101–104; Brooks, *Today's Health*, July, 1960, pp. 23–25; B. Smith, *American Heritage*, June, 1959, pp. 42–43; Jeanne Lodge, *American Mercury*, May, 1960, pp. 83–84; Paul Engle, *Reader's Digest*, July, 1959, pp. 149–150; W. Payne, *Saturday Evening Post*, Aug. 20, 1921, p. 16; H. I. Phillips, *Collier's*, July 2, 1927, p. 18.

10. *New York Times*, June 30, 1973, p. 30.

11. *New York Times*, May 19, 1974, p. 55; June 18, 1974, p. 16; April 13, 1975, p. 34; June 29, 1975, III, p. 15; July 2, 1975, p. 38; March 5, 1976, p. 33; March 28, 1978, p. 30.

12. *New York Times*, June 25, 1988, p. 18; July 3, 1978, B1; *Boston Globe*, May 4, 1988, p. 29.

13. "Americanization Day, A New Idea for July Fourth," *Survey*, March 29, 1915, p. 189; " Make the Fourth Americanization Day," *American City*, June 1915, pp. 492–3; "Proposal for Americanization Day," *Outlook*, June 30, 1915, p. 485; "Spread of Americanization Day Plans," *Survey*, June 19, 1915, p. 261; Sidney L. Gulick, "Make the Fourth Significant," *American City*, July 1914, pp. 23–24; *New York Times*, May 26, 1915, p. 8; Mrs. Percy V. Pennypacker, "An Ideal Fourth of July," *American City*, June, 1922, p. 627.

14. *New York Times*, July 5, 1924, p. 1.

Bicentennial   13

In 1966, President Lyndon Johnson appointed a 35-member American Revolution Bicentennial Commission, an act that excited profound lack of interest on the part of the American public. Everyone knew that the bicentennial of American Independence was approaching. Those few who had given the matter any thought assumed that something in the way of a world's fair would be organized to mark the occasion, something like the Philadelphia International Centennial Exhibition of 1876. But the nation's attention was riveted elsewhere.

American forces were mired in an Asian war that declined in popularity with every passing day. American youth were engaged in a massive rebellion against the beliefs and mores of their elders. And black Americans forcefully asserted their claim to full civil rights in a popular movement of unprecedented breadth and intensity. As the 1960s ended, the anti-Vietnam War movement, the youthful rebellion and the civil rights movement climaxed in violent riots and widespread civil disobedience that shook the nation to its foundation.

A String of Missteps, Squabbles and Poor Planning

A presidential election in 1968, a year when great cities erupted in violent protest and great men were assassinated, put Richard Milhous Nixon in the White House. The United States, which celebrated its centennial under the corrupt Grant administration, now prepared for its bicentennial under an administration that, for the only time in American history, saw first a vice president, then a president, resign in disgrace. All 35 members of the Bicentennial Commission, which had accomplished virtually nothing in the first two years of its existence, resigned after the election to be replaced by Nixon appointees. The latter addressed their efforts to adjudicating the squabble over which city would host the anticipated bicentennial exposition. Washington wanted the honor on the grounds that it is the nation's capital. Philadelphia and Boston claimed the right to host the fair because each was, in its way, the cradle of the Revolution. And Miami made a bid to hold the exposition, arguing that since southern Florida played no historic role in the revolution, its selection as the site for the bicentennial exhibition would please all of the other non-Revolutionary cities in the country.

While the debate over where to locate the exposition continued, Americans weighed in with suggestions for bicentennial commemorations of other sorts. Thought was given to honoring Independence by rebuilding a decayed American city, or by building a completely new city in an unpopulated area. Concern over the environment led to suggestions for environmental clean-ups, and for linking the 13 original states by high-speed rail. Some maintained that the nation ought to do something symbolizing world peace, like an international space mission, while others suggested that in the midst of pressing social, racial and environmental problems, the nation would do better to address itself to solving these problems than throw an expensive birthday party. Participants at a conference on world population control even suggested that America mark the bicentennial by setting an example for the world with a "pregnant pause."

Bombarded with frivolous and serious proposals, the Bicentennial Commission got nowhere on its central problem of where to locate the fair. To select one city was to disappoint three, a thing no politician likes to do. So, in 1970, the commissioners compromised by naming four bicentennial cities. This made four cities unhappy. How could any city mount a fair without federal money? Clearly there could not be four international exhibitions. Backpedaling in an effort to put the exhibition back on track and simultaneously allow President Nixon to present Pennsylvania's Republican Senator Hugh Scott with a political plum during an important reelection campaign, the Commission gave the exposition to Philadelphia. Citizens of Philadelphia immediately protested the siting of the fair, which had not been carefully planned.

For two years the city and the commissioners danced a *pas de deux* of incompetence, poor planning and political ineptitude. Failure at the local level to consider carefully the disadvantages of a particular site and to orchestrate public support and federal failure to follow through on financial commitments scuttled one plan after another until time ran out. In May of 1972, citing a lack of both time and money, the Commission admitted its failure to organize a bicentennial exposition and the nation lost patience.

The political hacks on the Bicentennial Commission, nearly all Republicans and administration loyalists, had squandered four years and tens of millions of dollars in planning that had produced no exposition and very little else. Private memos showing that the commissioners had worked hard to use the bicentennial to improve the president's image added to the administration's embarrassment and forced President Nixon to create a new American Revolution Bicentennial Administration which, it was hoped, would de-politicize the planning and produce appropriate bicentennial events.[1]

Grass-Roots Celebrations

The partisan agenda and ineptitude of the Nixon-appointed commissioners encouraged a preoccupied nation to neglect or reject all plans for large-scale bicentennial observances. Colorado, daunted by the necessarily large financial commitment, withdrew its bid to host the 1976 Olympic Games. And the much ballyhooed proposal to build a new national park in every state in honor of the bicentennial, an idea put forward by the Commission when it was unable to mount an exposition, never got off the ground. In marked contrast to 1876, when Philadelphians mounted a successful world's fair in the face of federal indifference, no city or state was willing to act without federal backing, and the federal government seemed unable to act. There would be no fair, no new buildings, no parks, no monuments. Beset by racial and generational strife, America lacked the will to plan a major celebration.

The new Bicentennial Administration, headed by former Navy secretary John Warner, made virtue out of necessity as it set out to plan a grass-roots bicentennial. Deprived of focal national events, the Bicentennial would be composed of hundreds of small-scale, local celebrations, with the Bicentennial Administration acting as a kind of clearinghouse to list the multitude of diverse events. Anything and everything could be included on the official list of Bicentennial events. "All you have to do is apply."[2]

The erection of a giant statue of a goose in Summer, Montana, "Wild Goose Capital of the World," was an official bicentennial event, as was a chili championship in San Marcos, Texas. Eager to produce major events of national scope, the administration worked hard to enlist large-scale corporate participation, but corporations were leary of participation. During the long years of the Vietnam War, patriotism had become downright unfashionable. Doubtful that red, white and blue events would prove popular with the American public, corporate leaders held back from making commitments to sponsor bicentennial programs in more than a token way.

When the first big corporation made a major commitment to sponsor an important, national-scale bicentennial event, the Bicentennial Administration held an official press conference in the main auditorium of the State Department to announce the breakthrough: Disneyland and Disney World were joining the Bicentennial. Parades at the theme parks would feature Betsy Ross stitching the first flag, costumed suffragettes, a first Thanksgiving float, a stagecoach, and Mickey, Donald and Goofy dressed up in tricorns and ruffled shirts in imitation of the piper, the drummer and the flagbearer in Archibald Willard's famous painting, "The Spirit of '76." A goodly supply of red, white and blue coffee mugs and new car ads with George Washington making the sales pitch were to be expected, but increasingly, the question was posed: Would there be anything else?

Serious work was done by the National Park Service, which renovated and restored a number of important historic sites, notably Independence Hall in Philadelphia, and scholarly works on the Revolutionary era were launched or published. But the bicentennial, as planned by the Nixon administration, was a thing of almost no substance and very little form. Fortunately, citizens' committees in many towns took the initiative to plan appropriate local commemorations.

Up and down the East Coast, bicentennial committees planned to celebrate the 200th anniversaries of their particular moments of Revolutionary glory. Reenactments of historic events were such a popular part of the Bicentennial that the limited geographical scope of the Revolution threatened to cause widespread dissappointment until planners realized that events could be detached from location. Creative planning enabled George Washington to cross Miami's Biscayne Bay, standing tall in a handsome uniform, his booted foot resting on the seat of a motorboat. And a full-dress battle was reenacted at Flushing Meadows Park in Queens, New York, a borough where no fighting took place during the Revolution.

Towns better endowed with Revolutionary history staged reenactments on the anniversary date and as close as they could manage to the site of the historical event. The burning of a replica of the British revenue cutter *Gaspee* took lace on schedule off Warwick, Rhode Island, June 10, 1972. And Boston, that hotbed of radical politics that so troubled King George, prepared to celebrate the bicentennial of its famous Tea Party.

At the original Boston Tea Party, a mob dressed to resemble Indians threw a shipment of tea into the harbor as a protest against taxation without representation. The reenactment, planned to be a quaint costume party, surprised its organizers by turning into a genuine political protest.

First, the Sierra Club protested the intentional pollution of Boston Harbor with tea leaves. Then the Boston Indian Council objected to the Indian costumes and the city agreed to stage the reenactment without tea, warpaint or feathered headresses. The Disabled American Veterans, who had reenacted the Tea Party annually for many years, complained about the restrictions and were allowed to appear in warpaint, on condition that they disappear before the official reenactment got under way.

On the morning of December 16, 200 years to the day after Sam Adams' liberty boys staged the original demonstration, the veterans appeared in "Indian" costume and dumped boxes of non-polluting maple leaves into the harbor. Then the official reenacters appeared in colonial garb, boarded the two-masted, replica brig, and threw empty boxes into the water shouting "Down with King George." Protesters in the crowd shouted, "Down with King Richard," referring to the increasing pressure President Richard Nixon was under to resign in the wake of scandals and loss of public confidence in his administration. The protest was staged by members of the People's Bicentennial Commission, who led a march from the wharf to Faneuil Hall, site of many historic protests, where an "impeachment town meeting" was held.

The People's Bicentennial Commission was a radical group headed by Jeremy Rifkin, an antiwar activist who had transferred the focus of his attention to the Bicentennial and was leading a nationwide effort to use it as the occasion for sweeping social and economic reform. The People's Commission called for the reduction of discrepancies in wealth and promoted an anti-business agenda, accusing corporations of destroying the environment, dodging taxes and manufacturing unemployment. One Boston policeman at the Tea Party muttered, "I thought this was over with the '60s," but the antiestablishment antics were undeniably in the spirit of Sam Adams and the Sons of Liberty.[3]

At a time when the administration in office was patently dishonest and out of step with the nation, and the official Bicentennial Administration devoted its efforts to encouraging commercial promotions but never said a word about the ideals for which the Revolution was fought, the People's Commission provided a welcome infusion of idealism.

The Bicentennial Year

The American Revolution was fought by people who demanded the right of representative government under a system of just laws, people willing to stand up and even to die for ideas they believed in. Its bicentennial was planned as a series of battle reenactments and commemorative-edition china plates. Small wonder that Americans paid some attention to a group that spoke feelingly about the ideals of the Founding Fathers, even though the rhetoric of the People's Bicentennial Commission interpreted those ideas through a Marxist lens. America wanted to hear its leaders speak about the ideas on which the republic was founded, ideas that were worth fighting for in 1776 and worth cheering for in 1976. When neither the president nor his administration were able to articulate those ideas, Americans stood up and cheered anyway. Much of the Bicentennial that resulted was a little silly, but it was enthusiastic.

The crowned heads of Europe came to call, notably Elizabeth II, great-great-great-great-grandaughter of that "tyrant," George III, and the American Revolution Bicentennial Administration finally pulled itself together to send a bicentennial exhibition chugging across the country in a 12-car train pulled by a red, white and blue steam locomotive. Americans everywhere hung out flags and painted fire hydrants to resemble small versions of Uncle Sam, or little red, white and blue Continental soldiers. Wagon trains crossed the plains heading east to Valley Forge, hundreds of mountain climbers scaled Mt. McKinley, and the spaceship Viking landed on Mars as the decade-long celebration peaked in the summer of 1976 on a note of exultation.

The People's Bicentennial Commission, which set out to usher in a revolution that would reorganize the economy and bring the working people into power, instead represented the last gasp of 1960s-style political activism. The Vietnam War was over, black citizens had made monumental strides toward equal rights, the generation gap was receding into history, and a nation that had been chagrined by the resignations of Vice President Spiro Agnew and President Richard Nixon, celebrated its bicentennial under the honorable and respected President Gerald Ford. More significantly, the political system demonstrated its continued health in a series of primary elections that awarded the Democratic nomination for president to Governor Jimmy Carter of Georgia. In the summer of 1976, America was calmer and more hopeful than it had been for many years.

Sunrise on the nation's 200th birthday came first to the tiny, potato-growing town of Mars Hill, Maine, where National Guardsmen fired a 50-gun salute and raised the American flag. At two in the afternoon, Eastern Standard Time, bells rang out across the land, as communities large and small marked the bicentennial of the glorious day when 13 colonies became a nation.

Bristol, Rhode Island celebrated with a parade, as it has done every year since 1786. Newport, Rhode Island planted a young buttonwood Liberty Tree beside the tree planted at the Centennial on the spot where British troops chopped down the original. Boston turned out, as it does every year, to hear the Boston Pops Orchestra play Tchaikovsky's 1812 Overture, punctuated by blasts from 105-mm howitzers and bells hanging in the nearby Church of the Advent.

Philadelphia and Atlanta staged impressive parades. Seventeen hundred and seventy-six new citizens were naturalized at Chicago Stadium and St. Louis watched an air show at the Gateway Arch. Three churches in Evergreen, Alabama held a parade and gospel show to protest racial bigotry; residents of George, Washington baked and sliced the largest cherry pie in history; and citizens of American Samoa came to Pago Pago to watch boat races and a pole-climbing contest. Some of the observances were serious, some were frivolous and some, like the 33.5 tons of fireworks set off at the Washington Monument, were out-and-out dazzling.

Despite the failures of the national government and Bicentennial Administration, the efforts of millions of citizens made the Bicentennial a smashing success. In every state, historic buildings were refurbished, parks were dedicated, reenactments were staged in honor of the event. Museums mounted historical exhibitions, orchestras performed patriotic music and theaters staged appropriate plays. Television joined the celebration with historical specials and "Bicentennial Minute" advertising spots, which made up in zeal some of what they lacked in the way of historical accuracy. In the spirit of this genuinely spontaneous outpouring of Bicentennial enthusiasm, the event that turned out to be the centerpiece of the Bicentennial was not the work of any governmental or official commission, but the effort of a private citizen with an idea.

The Triumph of the Tall Ships

Frank O. Braynard, an author, historian and founder of the South Street Seaport, had been chairman of "Op Sail '64," at the New York World's Fair. A man who loved ships and the sea, he dreamed of marking the Bicentennial with a great gathering of sailing ships and, in 1971, set out to make his dream come true. Braynard enlisted Emil Mossbacher, Jr., defender of the America's Cup, as chairman, and with a small committee and an infinitesimal budget, began to issue invitations to what would be the biggest gathering of sailing ships since the British, Russian and French navies defeated Egyptian and Turkish fleets at the Battle of Navarino in 1827.

On the Fourth of July 1976, as President Gerald Ford, Vice President Nelson Rockefeller and 3,000 dignitaries watched from the deck of the aircraft carrier *Forrestal*, the tall ships sailed into New York Harbor. Six million Americans crowded the shoreline to witness the stately procession, along with the crews of 50 warships under the flags of 23 nations; the entire country watched on television. The crowd was joyful, the ships magnificent, the moment of celebration perfect.

The largest ships, 18 square-riggers, were training ships crewed by naval cadets and young merchant marine seamen. Most of them arrived in New York at the end of a three-legged race, from Plymouth, England to Tenerife in the

The Spanish training ship, Juan Sebastian de Elcano, enters New York Harbor under full sail in the parade of tall ships on the Bicentennial Fourth. Pleasure boats dot the harbor and spectators crowd the Brooklyn waterfront to witness the spectacle as a New York City fireboat shoots its hoses into the air in a salute to the holiday. (Photo credit: Courtesy of South Street Seaport)

Canary Islands, from the Canaries to Bermuda, then on to Newport, Rhode Island, where the crew and ships were admired by crowds of thousands.

New York feted the sailors handsomely, showering them with receptions and tours and friendship, as the city that had so reluctantly joined the Revolution hosted its bicentennial birthday party. There was a parade in Washington. In Boston the Declaration of Independence was read from the balcony of the Old State House. And President Ford delivered a suitable oration in Philadelphia, before heading for New York Harbor in a helicopter. But, on the bicentennial Fourth of July, the eyes of the nation were on New York.

There, under the upraised lantern of the Statue of Liberty, 220 sailing ships from 31 countries passed in stately procession up the Hudson River in graceful salute to a nation founded upon the right of men and women to govern themselves.

Notes

1. *New York Times*, Dec. 1, 1973, p. 36; Dec. 14, 1973, p. 46.
2. *New York Times*, Feb. 17, 1975, p. 45; American Revolution Bicentennial Administration, *Official Master List of Bicentennial Activities*, Government Printing Office, Washington, D.C., 1975.
3. "The Tea Party Tempest," *Newsweek*, Dec. 31, 1973, pp. 11–12; *New York Times*, June 18, 1976; William Randel, "The Fife and Drum of Big Business," *The Nation*, Jan. 22, 1973, pp. 108–110; Robert Karen, "New Light in the Steeple," *The Nation*, June 29, 1974; "Spirit of '76," *National Review*, March 19, 1976, p. 256; People's Bicentennial Commission, *America's Birthday*, Simon and Schuster, 1975.

Epilogue: Statue of Liberty Centennial

In 1986 the great Statue of Liberty in New York Harbor (originally known as *Liberty Enlightening the World*) turned 100 years old, and America celebrated with a Fourth of July extravaganza.[1]

Frederic Auguste Bartholdi's massive sculpture of a female Liberty had been commissioned by moderate French Republicans in 1871 as a centennial gift to the republican United States. Intended as an attention-getting ploy to promote republican doctrines during a confused period of French politics, it mattered little to Liberty's French sponsors that Americans were not at all sure that they wanted the oversized figure.[2] It took more than a decade to cultivate enough public favor in Liberty's new country to raise the funds needed to build a pedestal and erect the statue on Liberty Island, but she was finally ready to be unveiled on a wet, foggy October afternoon in 1886—in time to greet the millions of new Americans who would sail into New York Harbor during the great wave of immigration from the 1880s until World War I. To these people, the sight of the Statue of Liberty promised freedom from the political, religious and class oppression of their European homelands. Her torch held out a beacon of hope to welcome them to their new land.

Immigrants landed on nearby Ellis Island, where they were processed in cavernous buildings that had fallen into disrepair after they were last used in the 1950s. When it became apparent that the Statue itself needed extensive repairs, the National Park Service decided to raise funds to completely restore the Statue of Liberty and make Ellis Island into a monument to the millions of immigrants who built America.

Lee Iacocca, a businessman and the son of Italian immigrants who became a national folk hero following his successful turnaround of the failing Chrysler Corporation, was tapped to head up the Statue of Liberty Advisory Commission, which was charged with planning the futures of the Liberty and Ellis Island monuments. He was also in charge of the private fund-raising effort that paid for the restorations and planned the Independence Day ceremonies in honor of the statue's 1986 centennial. Iacocca succeeded in raising $250 million with such skill and enthusisam that rumors circulated of a candidacy for president in 1988. His efforts resulted in an extensive restoration program for the two monuments that began in 1982. The statue was veiled by scaffolding for nearly three years while it was renovated for its 1986, centennial; improvements included a glass- walled hydraulic elevator to the top of the statue and a new museum. (The detailed restoration of the Ellis Island complex is expected to conclude by the time of its own centennial in 1992.) In the spring of 1986, with plans for a Fourth of July gala well under way and the $66 million renovation of the statue itself nearly complete, Interior Secretary Donald Hodel asked Iacocca to step down as chairman of the Advisory Commission (though he continued as head of the private effort). Iacocca had wanted the whole of Ellis Island as a museum and memorial, almost as a shrine to the immigrant generations. Secretary Hodel, faced with the economic realities of running national parks, wanted part of the island to be the site of a hotel and conference center.

America was prosperous in 1986 and in a mood of self-congratulation. That summer, the Statue of Liberty seemed to be everywhere. She attended costume parties and rode in Fourth of July parades, she appeared in magazines, on television and in political campaigns, and on the Fourth of July weekend, millions of people walked around New York City wearing green foam rubber hats in the shape of Liberty's crown.

The extravaganza Mr. Iacocca and his committee had planned to celebrate Independence and Liberty could not be contained within the confines of 24 hours. It began on Thursday morning, July third, with the ringing of church bells, mass at New York's St. Patrick's Cathedral, and a parade of small sailing ships, and continued full tilt for four days.

On Thursday evening, watched by President Mitterrand of France and other dignitaries, President Reagan "unveiled" the statue by pushing a light switch igniting 1.4 million watts of laser beams that shot across the harbor bathing the statue in increasing washes of light. Beams of red caught the base first, then red-amber on the pedestal, then steel blue lights revealed the statue itself. Following the washes of color, 15 floodlights illuminated the statue in brilliant white light.

With the statue visible in New York Harbor and on the television screens of the nation, 25,000 immigrants took the oath of naturalized citizenship at 44 sites around the country, including 14,000 in the Orange Bowl at Miami. Two hundred and seventy-six immigrants representing 31 states and 100 countries of origin were naturalized by Chief Justice Warren Burger on Liberty Island, where the ceremony was accompanied by music and speeches. Then, at 11:00 P.M. the statue's torch was relit and the crowd watched a brief, dazzling display of red, white and blue fireworks.

Morning broke cool and clear over the great port city on the Fourth of July. President Reagan steamed down the Hudson on the battleship *Iowa*, receiving 21-gun salutes from a flotilla of 44 ships from American and foreign naval ships. The three-masted Coast Guard sailing ship *Eagle* entered New York Harbor through the Narrows at the head of a parade of sailing ships that would continue all day long. Two New York City fireboats preceeded the *Eagle* into the harbor firing hose salutes. Just past Governor's Island the fireboats veered off, and the crowd on Manhattan's Battery saw the *Eagle* come out of the mist like a ghost ship emerging from another era.

Small matter that the ships proceeded under power, their sails luffing in light winds that blew from the wrong direction; the parade was magnificent. The millions of New Yorkers who watched from shore or from boats in the harbor, and the tens of millions who watched on television around the world, were stirred by this awesome vision of the bygone age of sail.

At 8:00 P.M. the Boston Pops, which had raised hackles in Boston by skipping its traditional Independence Day concert on the city's Esplanade to participate in Liberty Weekend in New York, played an All-American Concert featuring works by Gershwin, Cohan, Sousa and others, at Liberty State Park in New Jersey. Boston was not alone in feeling bereft that Fourth of July. Across the nation, Americans who perceived nothing special being done in their hometowns to celebrate the holiday, spent the weekend watching televised accounts of the celebration in New York City.

That celebration culminated on Friday evening with the largest display of fireworks in American history. Forty thousand shells burst over New York harbor in a spectacular display that lasted for half an hour. It was glorious tribute to Liberty, who, after 100 years, still illuminated the hopes of world.

Notes

1. *A Celebration of Freedom; Liberty Weekend, 1986*, Liberty Centennial Press, New York, 1986; and newspaper and magazine accounts.
2. Marvin Trachtenberg, *The Statue of Liberty*, Viking Press, New York, 1976.

INDEX